199

 **St. Louis Community
College**

Forest Park
Florissant Valley
Meramec

Instructional Resources
St. Louis, Missouri

Terrence McNally

CASEBOOKS ON MODERN DRAMATISTS
VOLUME 22
GARLAND REFERENCE LIBRARY OF THE HUMANITIES
VOLUME 1933

CASEBOOKS ON MODERN DRAMATISTS
KIMBALL KING, *General Editor*

TERRENCE MCNALLY
A CASEBOOK

EDITED BY
TOBY SILVERMAN ZINMAN

GARLAND PUBLISHING, INC.
NEW YORK AND LONDON
1997

Library of Congress Cataloging-in-Publication Data

Terrence McNally : a casebook / edited by Toby Silverman Zinman.
        p.   cm. — (Garland reference library of the humanities ; v. 1933.
Casebooks on modern dramatists ; v. 22)
        Includes bibliographical references and index.
        ISBN 0-8153-2100-7 (alk. paper)
        1. McNally, Terrence—Criticism and interpretation.   I. Zinman, Toby
Silverman, 1942–   . II. Series: Garland reference library of the humanities ;
vol. 1933. III. Series: Garland reference library of the humanities.
Casebooks on modern dramatists ; vol. 22.
PS3563.A323Z88   1997
812'.54—dc21   96–45085
                                                                                    CIP

Cover photograph of Terrence McNally © Susan Johann.

Printed on acid-free, 250-year-life paper
Manufactured in the United States of America

For my daughter, Phoebe

Contents

General Editor's Note

Beginning with *And Things That Go Bump in the Night*, written when he was only twenty-three, Terrence McNally has been a prolific and controversial playwright for three decades, admired by theater audiences well as by academicians. He has garnered his share of Tony awards and several of his later works, especially *A Perfect Ganesh*, *Love! Valour! Compassion!* and *Master Class* are now considered "mainstream" American plays.

Toby Silverman Zinman is the perfect scholar to assemble a collection of essays on McNally. Just as she had the full cooperation of Rabe in her previous Garland volume, *David Rabe: A Casebook* (1991), Zinman received advice from McNally, and the volume includes her interviews with him and two of his major actors, Zoe Caldwell and Nathan Lane. A professor of English at the University of the Arts in Philadelphia, she is respected for her direction of Summer Seminars of Samuel Beckett's plays for the National Endowment for the Humanities, and she has written many articles for publication in periodicals like *Modern Drama* and *Theatre Journal*. She reviews Philadelphia theatre for *Variety* and *City Paper* and is a frequent contributor to *American Theater* magazine. In this volume, she offers students, critics, and admirers of McNally's work a panoply of his ideas and achievements.

Kimball King

Introduction

Terrence McNally's life in the theatre began when, at the age of twenty-three, he opened his first play, *And Things That Go Bump in the Night*, at the Guthrie Theatre and then on Broadway to scandalized and disastrous reviews. Since then he has won Tony after Tony, prize after prize, achieving a significant position in American drama, both on Broadway and Off. Through more than three decades of a career that continues to be prolific and progressively more serious, his plays have been death haunted and music vitalized.

Music is the abiding passion of McNally's life and work. His earliest journeyman work was on an adaptation of *The Lady of the Camellias* (1963)—which is, of course, the same Dumas story Verdi used for *La Traviata;* the characters in *And Things That Go Bump* are named for opera characters; *Frankie and Johnny in the Clair de Lune* (1987) opens with Bach and closes with Debussy. *The Lisbon Traviata* is, of course, filled with opera, as is *Master Class*. The opening stage directions of Act One of *Lips Together, Teeth Apart* (1991) is a perfect example of how crucial music is to McNally's dramatic imagination:

At rise, tableau*; Sally painting at an easel; Chloe standing at the kitchen sink, within; John reading a newspaper; Sam testing the chlorine level of the pool.*

No one moves. Silence.

Music begins: the farewell trio from Mozart's Cosi fan tutte.

As the trio progresses, the stage and the actors will slowly come to "life."

The first movement will be the gentle stirrings of an ornamental flag in the early-morning breeze.

Then SALLY will begin to paint, CHLOE to drink coffee in the kitchen, JOHN to turn the pages of his New York Times, *SAM to retrieve the chlorine indicator—but all in time to the music, not reaching naturalistic behavior until the end of the piece.*

By the time the trio ends, we will be in "real" time.

It is as though music is the life force, that which precedes the theatrical givens of speech and gesture.

And if music is the redemptive, invigorating force, death is always the fact, the point of a play's departure, that which makes not only the action of the play but the writing of the play necessary. Just as the death of her brother brought Sally and the three others to the inherited beach house on Fire Island for the Fourth of July holiday, so the play begins with a musical farewell. The plot of *A Perfect Ganesh* (1993) is generated by the two women's secret sorrows over the deaths of their sons, and their grief, however obliquely, generates the trip to India which is the action of the play. (As of this writing, McNally is working on a screenplay of *A Perfect Ganesh* for Merchant Ivory Productions, although he has no say about casting or final approval of the screenplay; as he put it: "They could read mine, think it was terrible and say, let's give it to Sam Shepard to rewrite. That's the huge difference between writing a play and writing a screenplay—you write a play on spec, but when it's done, every word in it is yours. When you write for Hollywood, they give you a lot of money up front, but what comes out on the screen you might not want to have any responsibility for. I think it's a fair tradeoff.") Benilde Montgomery's essay on *A Perfect Ganesh* illuminates the play by discussing its roots in the myth and religion of India, and in his essay on *Lips Together, Teeth Apart*, Stephen Watt discusses McNally as a postmodernist in light of current critical theory.

The early one-acts were products of their times: the anti-war plays, like *Botticelli* (1968), *Bringing It All Back Home* (1969), and the anti-establishment protest plays, like *Next* (1967), *¡Cuba Si!*

(1968) and *Witness* (1968), all suggest that McNally is not at heart a political playwright. Howard Stein, in his essay on the early plays, discusses *And Things That Go Bump in the Night*, the subsequent one-acts, and the final play of that first stage of his career, *Where Has Tommy Flowers Gone?* (1971), concluding that the radical promise of the first work was not fulfilled.

McNally has not relinquished his affection for the one-act, and *Prelude and Leibestod* (1989), a hilarious, horrifying theatrical aria, and *Andre's Mother* (1988), which was subsequently revised and lengthened for television and for which he won a 1990 Emmy, show how his skill with the short form has grown. His newest one-act, which opened Off-Broadway in June of 1996 is "Dusk," one of three short plays under the umbrella title of *By the Sea, by the Sea, by the Beautiful Sea* (the others are by Joe Pintauro, "Dawn," and Lanford Wilson, "Day"). It is not yet published.

Much of the second stage of McNally's career was devoted to farce—particularly sex farce—and the theme of homosexuality which had lurked in the earliest plays now moves downstage, but farce is farce, after all, and McNally is, at this point, not attempting to convey gay life authentically for a straight audience. *Whiskey* (1973), *Bad Habits* (1974), and *The Ritz* (1975) are all entertaining, but they shun the intimacy and gravity which now seem to be the keynotes of McNally's best work, although despite the growing seriousness of the dramas, the dialogue is always filled with laugh lines and wit. McNally's characters are always funny if not happy, and always articulate and self-aware.

After the deaths of his "two best friends and dearest collaborators" ("A Few Words," xi), Robert Drivas and James Coco, McNally wrote *Frankie and Johnny in the Clair de Lune* (1987). McNally's own screenplays for *Frankie and Johnny in the Clair de Lune* and *The Ritz* raise problematic issues of evisceration which Helen Buttel addresses in her essay on the adaptations.

The Lisbon Traviata (1985, revised 1989) is pivotal in McNally's transformation into a mature and contemplative theatrical voice. This is the first of the longer plays about complex relationships among more fully-developed characters who are often desperate, damaged people. It is also the first of the plays which not only uses music but is *about* music, and Sam Abel's essay on the complicated history of this play's conclusion—to murder or not to murder—is richly informed by the critic's own extensive knowledge of opera.

Love! Valour! Compassion! is, like the earlier work, death soaked and music redeemed. Although McNally is not in the avant-garde or on the cutting edge—despite the fact that his *Sweet Eros* in 1969 brought nudity to Off-Broadway (before the far more sensational *Che!* and *Oh! Calcutta*)—*Love! Valour! Compassion!* (1994) generated huge critical controversy both within and without the gay community (with much critical ink spilled on its use of male nudity). Although much of the debate has centered on where this play falls in the history of gay theatre, as do the two essays in this volume, I hope this will not become the exclusive view of *Love! Valour! Compassion!* John Clum and Steven Drukman come to surprisingly similar conclusions although these critics often write from opposing poles in the sexual politics of gay/queer theory. I have included an interview with Nathan Lane who played Buzz in *Love! Valour! Compassion!*; McNally considers Lane his foremost interpreter and has written a number of roles for him.

Master Class is about Maria Callas, the great diva, and the legendary master classes she held at Juilliard in the early 1970s. It is interesting that McNally himself taught playwriting at Juilliard last year and used his own work-in-progress—the early script of *Master Class*—to teach *his* master classes. McNally is well known as an expert on opera, and he is frequently heard introducing the Metropolitan Opera radio broadcasts—another lovely completion of another lovely loop, since it was on those radio broadcasts that McNally, as a boy in Texas, first heard Callas sing.

I have provided McNally's comments on Callas—extracted from the interviews—as a preface to Cary Mazer's groundbreaking essay on the play, John Ardoin's authoritative essay on Maria Callas, and Zoe Caldwell's conversation, in another interview, about playing Maria Callas in the world premiere of *Master Class*.

As of this writing, McNally has just finished the book for a musical adaptation of Doctorow's novel, *Ragtime* (score by Lynn Ahrens and Stephen Flaherty), which opens in Toronto in December of 1996 and which, at press time, he expects to open in New York a year later. *Love! Valour! Compassion!* is being filmed with the original cast, directed by Joe Mantello (who directed the original stage production) in Montreal where, McNally told me, they had found the ideal house. Most exciting is the news that a new play will open at the Manhattan Theatre Club in the spring of 1997—McNally is keeping the title and subject a secret.

It gives me pleasure to thank everyone who contributed to this volume. Thanks, too, to Kimball King, the general editor of this series, for letting me do it again, and to Chuck Bartelt, the computer wizard at Garland, without whose help I would have been stranded. I am grateful to Zoe Caldwell and Nathan Lane for taking time to talk with me and for the great pleasure their performances have given me. Finally, I am beholden to Terrence McNally, not only for the hours he spent talking with me, but for many fine evenings in the theatre.

T.S.Z.
June 1996

Chronology

1939   Terrence McNally is born 3 November, in St. Petersburg, Florida, son of Hubert Arthur and Dorothy Katharine (Rapp) McNally. In early childhood, the family moves to Corpus Christi, Texas, where his father operated a beer distributorship.

1956–60   Columbia University, journalism major. Works several summers as reporter on the *Corpus Christi Caller-Times*.

1960   Graduates with B.A. from Columbia University, Phi Beta Kappa. Awarded Columbia University Henry Evans Travelling Fellowship. Spends six months in Puerto Vallarta, Mexico. Sends play to Molly Kazan, wife of Elia Kazan, at Actor's Studio in New York.

1961   Stage Manager, Actor's Studio.

1961–62   World tour with the John Steinbeck family as tutor-companion to the two Steinbeck sons.

1962   Stanley Award for "This Side of the Door."

1963–65   Film critic, *Seventh Art*, New York.

1965–66   Assistant editor, *Columbia College Today*, New York.

1966   Guggenheim Fellowship.

1969   Guggenheim Fellowship.
            Runner-up Drama Desk Award for most promising playwright.

1974   Hull-Warriner Award for *Bad Habits*. Most Distinguished
        Play, Obie Award for *The Ritz*.

1981   Vice-president of Dramatists Guild, an office he still
        holds.

1987   Hull-Warriner Award for *Frankie and Johnny in the Clair
        de Lune*.

1989   Hull-Warriner Award for *The Lisbon Traviata*.

1990   Emmy Award for Best Writing in a Miniseries or a
        Special for *Andre's Mother*.

1993   Tony Award for Best Book of a Musical for *Kiss of the
        Spider Woman* (score by Kander and Ebb).

1995   *Love! Valour! Compassion!* wins Tony Award for Best Play,
        Outer Critics Circle Award, the Drama Desk Award and
        The New York Drama Critics Circle Award for Best
        American Play. Named "Person of the Year" by the Na-
        tional Theatre Conference for his contribution to Ameri-
        can theatre.

1996   *Master Class* wins Tony Award for Best Play, [Philadelphia's]
        Barrymore Award for Best Play, [Los Angeles's] Ovation
        Award.

Terrence McNally

Chapter One
Interview with Terrence McNally

Toby Silverman Zinman

Editor's Note: Terrence McNally and I first spoke on November 7, 1994, a week after Love! Valour! Compassion! *opened, when he had come to Philadelphia to address a Playwrights' symposium. The Philadelphia Theatre Company would be premiering* Master Class *in March of 1995, so both of those plays were naturally very much on his mind. We spoke again at the Manhattan Theatre Club on December 9, 1994; both these long conversations (of many hours each) have been combined. McNally's comments on* Master Class *have been extracted and preface the essays in this book which deal with that play.*

TZ: Music is obviously so important to you—in *Lisbon Traviata* and certainly in this new play [*Master Class*—which at this point I had only read in typescript]. Do you wish you wrote operas instead of plays? Does this new play aspire to an operatic state?

TMcN: If I were a composer, I would write opera—opera is certainly an influence on my work. It was certainly one of the ways I became attracted to theatre and attempted to make sense of the human experience which I think is, by definition what art is, to try to explain what it's like to be alive, or in love, or what joy is. The biggest influences on me as a child were opera and musical comedy. The Metropolitan Opera existed on the radio, I fell in love with opera in the sixth grade; I was at a Catholic school and a nun played Puccini love duets for us, and I liked it right away. The way most people like strawberry ice cream cones—that's how it was for me with Italian opera. Not all opera, of course; it took me a while before I enjoyed Mozart and Wagner. When I was much much younger, about five or six, my parents took me to see *Annie Get Your Gun,* and then when I was twelve my parents took me to see *The King and I* with Gertrude Lawrence, and those were the only two theatre experiences I had as a child—both were on trips to New York. But the opera was something I was able to fantasize and dream about because of the Texaco broadcasts, and I used to build little sets in the little theatre I made. But I never connected any of this to playwriting or theatre—I don't know what I thought it was.

I surely did not want to be a playwright until I came to New York and started to go to the theatre—much, much later. Maybe my senior year in college it occurred to me to write a play. Opera was something I enjoyed passively—I think I'm a very good listener—I participate with my body, I twist and turn in my seat, but I can't play the piano, I can't sing, so opera is something I can enjoy passively. After seeing those musicals I certainly never said, I want to write a play, they weren't something I could participate in, but they're obviously very important to me as an influence. That's how I knew what it was like to sit in a dark room and be transported, taken somewhere else. I've only worked on two musicals and those fairly late in my career—*The Rink*, the first show I did with Kandor and Ebb, is only about eight years ago, and then *Kiss of the Spider Woman* was only two years ago.

TZ: You say that opera made you know what it was like to be alive—that's a very extravagant take on the human condition, so lavish and extreme.

TMcN: Well, I think my plays *are* lavish and extreme—I'm not a naturalistic writer—I think sometimes I'm operatic, but to me my aesthetic of theatre is influenced by these early experiences. My plays are sometimes operatic, there are arias, there are duets—*Lips Together* is my most operatic play—Mozart even opened the play. And now when I see it or read it I say, My God, these are quartets, or trios or duets. My early plays are all arias.

Love! Valour! is the least musical—that is, there's less music in it—they sing at the beginning of each act, but I chose it because I like the idea of seven men singing *a capella,* and Stephen Foster's music I enjoy—it's welcoming, it's friendly music, and it seemed the right way to open the play. Some of my early plays have more references to music—actually *Lips Together* has many more than this play. Music, opera is not naturalistic. If we listen to *Traviata*, we know that people don't sing in real life, but a good performance of *La Traviata*, such as the one I heard Maria Callas give at the Met, moves you in a way that is timeless and absolutely up to the moment. So I take opera very seriously, and I think art should inspire. So although I take theatre very seriously, one may not always achieve that level of intensity.

I suppose I have to grit my teeth and refer to my plays as "comedies," which I get a little tired of, but people do like handles I suppose, and I think there's laughter in my plays, and I think I have a comic sensibility, but I don't think I write comedies.

I think my plays are plays, which implies a certain artificiality. I was surprised that so many people referred to *Frankie and Johnny* as a naturalistic play, which I don't think it is at all. I think it's the most poetic play I've ever written, but because they made real sandwiches and made a western omelet in the second act, people think it's naturalistic, but it's not. That's why opera is important—it's not naturalistic.

The two musical comedies I saw had two extraordinary star performers, Ethel Merman and Gertrude Lawrence, and my work is best served by actors who are (and this is not a pejorative word) *performers* and less well served by intensely "Method" actors. I found my true artistic collaborator in Nathan Lane or Kathy Bates—actors who find the feeling in the lines without having to add "uhs," "you knows," "I means"—and just go with the language. They say the words and the feeling follows. So many actors have to have the feeling before they can say the line—it's not my music. I believe very profoundly that there are McNally actors, just as there are Guare actors or Mamet actors, actors who serve my vision. In this last play I very much found a McNally director—Joe Mantello—I am rapturous about how beautifully served I am by this production [of *Love! Valour! Compassion!*]. As a director he has found the larger thing I'm writing about. The set for the play is nonexistent; it's a place you can act in, yet it becomes all things—lakeside, the interior of house, it moves with fluidity. The designer, Loy Arcenas, found the poetic metaphoric space which I could only describe haltingly in the first stage directions as "bare stages"—but he knew what I meant. I didn't want real rooms with beds and chairs—the whole first speech is describing a house the audience can't see. Other directors wanted to get a horsehair sofa there, but I didn't want a sofa; I wanted what that sofa meant to that man.

I don't think I'm any more modest or immodest than any other playwright, but I do think we're vastly overpraised when a play works, since it's such an elaborate collaboration. Without the right director and designers, a play is dead in the water. It's nice when you have a successful play to get a lot of praise, but it has to be shared with other people.

[I mention the swan ballet in *Love! Valour! Compassion!*]

TMcN: That's the sort of theatre moment you live for—I thought it would work, but they were standing there in their tutus and then the lighting designer brought up those footlights, and they suddenly looked like Degas ballerinas. The costume designer gave them those little headbands. It's the most absurd-looking moment in the play. It begins with great hilarity, and then—it's just a wonderful section in which I feel I can't do better than that as a writer or find better collaborators than this.

Two days before we started [*Love! Valour! Compassion!*] we still didn't have the full cast. I had been willing to cast months earlier because I was getting lazy and panicked and I wanted to go away for the summer, but I spent the summer in New York seeing actors. It was supposed to have been the last play of last season, but if we had done it then, it would not have had Nathan Lane or Stephen Spinella or Joe—I don't think he could have done this and been in *Angels* [*in America*—in which Mantello played Louis Ironson in the Broadway production].

So few theatre people go to the theatre. I go to the theatre three times a week or so. People see *Love! Valour! Compassion!* and say, how can I get Joe Mantello? Six months ago, it was Joe Mantello, who are you? I'd seen three plays the man had directed and I thought he was extraordinary. So I'm smart that way.

TZ: Would you talk some more about your ideas about acting and how they relate to playwriting?

TMcN: American acting went through a period when it was so involved with "inner truth"—but the truth of the actor not the truth of the character. If there was a kind of decline in our theatre, it might have been that the actors were not rising to the plays. The Actors Studio had a playwrights unit, but no great plays came out of it. I think the inner truth of Blanche DuBois is important, not the inner truth of the actress playing her.

I have always responded to technique—an actor who will cry on cue, even if it's pure technique that's making him cry. We went through a period of theatre being contemptuous of craft—in playwriting too—and I think our generation of writers went through a period of being overpraised for anything we wrote. In the sixties, if you wrote a play and you were under thirty, you could get it done in New York. A lot of young American writers were overpraised and never developed a sufficient technique in playwriting, so when your youth is gone, what are you going to do? I'm a great believer in technique, and I'm sorry it's such a dirty word.

I think a lot of young people today are writing plays who don't know what a good play is—they read *Streetcar, Long Day's Journey, Death of a Salesman* and that's it—one play by each playwright, what's the biggest hit, what's the easiest to rent the video of—there's no respect for the body of work or for the man. *Streetcar* is just the play that made Marlon Brando a star.

I've been teaching, and students are very resistant to talking about craft in playwriting. It's not enough to write what you feel—it's what they tell singers, "Don't sing on your capital, sing on your interest." I find that young people say, "I don't know what to write about." That's like saying, "I'm bored." I couldn't possibly live long enough to write all the plays I dream of writing. It's slower each time, and I guess as I get older I'm unwilling to be alone for the period of time it takes to write them and see them into production. It's very lonely—like a boat drifting out, in the sense that once you really begin to write a play, you're really not participating in society; you may be with people, but you're really not listening to them. I just can't imagine saying I don't know what to write about.

TZ: What happens once the play is finished?

TMcN: I do a lot of work in rehearsal—that's too long, that's too short, that's not funny, that's not clear. Joe Mantello was very helpful editing *Love! Valour! Compassion!* I had trouble ending it, and he took the last eight lines and moved them a page earlier—made an enormous difference. You needed the information in those eight lines, but it had never occurred to me to move them. By the time a play opens, the cast knows the characters better than you do—some of the best lines and scenes were not there in the original version—a lot of my work is in the first few weeks of rehearsal—they inspired me to write them. If you just wrote it all by yourself, then why bother to go to rehearsal if you're not going to change anything?

TZ: So collaboration is important to you?

TMcN: I accept that theatre is a collaboration. Edward Albee called me the other day and said, "You're such a goody-two-shoes. I just read some interview where you said theatre's a collaboration. Do you really believe that?" And I said, "Yes, I really do. And you really don't, do you?" And he said, "No, I don't."

I think being a playwright is being 100% responsible for what happens on stage, which means acknowledging what other people have done. If you're the playwright, your name is on the set; it's on the lighting; it's on the costumes—It's not enough to say here's the script, I hope they'll do it right. And you have to learn—only Nathan could have taken that line in *Love! Valour! Compassion!* about having a boyfriend and hollered to the audience, "which I don't." There's the lonely part, writing it, and then you get to play with all these fabulously talented people—and I've been lucky, working with really great actors.

[Kathy Bates, who starred in *Frankie and Johnny in the Clair de Lune,* is one of the few actors McNally considers his ideal interpreters; this short list of actors, including Zoe Caldwell, is headed by Nathan Lane (an interview with him appears with the essays on *Love! Valour! Compassion!* since he was starring in that show at that time). F. Murray Abraham, for whom McNally wrote *Frankie and*

Johnny and who had been in four of his plays, has not worked with McNally since a scheduling change combined with a movie commitment forced him out of *Frankie and Johnny*. ("And he hasn't spoken to me since. It just seems silly to get mad.") Abraham got his original McNally role as Tommy Flowers at an open casting call. McNally affectionately tells the story of how Abraham came to the audition straight from the airport, having just gotten off a plane from Rome, and still had his suitcase with him. He was told the audition was only for actors with agents. He just waited all day until 7 P.M., and finally McNally let him read. "He read three lines and I said, "It's yours." "He did four of my plays in a row—I wrote *Bad Habits* specifically for him and the part of Chris in *The Ritz*, which he was brilliant in."]

TZ: In *Master Class* you have Callas say, "Words mean something. Vowels are the inarticulate sounds our hearts make. 'Oh.' Consonants give them specific meaning." Do you feel that way about English?

TMcN: Yes—not when I'm talking to you but on stage, in the theatre. That's one of the reasons I respond to an actor like Nathan—he relishes each word—so many actors don't delight in language, it's just "what are my lines?" and they say the words—not "what a wonderful rhythm this has" or "how interesting"—and my work especially seems to bring out something in him. I hadn't seen *Love! Valour! Compassion!* in quite a while, and I went back and watched the third act—Nathan was better than I'd ever seen him, it was incredibly emotional, he had the whole audience sobbing, but it wasn't a new performance either, if you know what I mean—he hadn't changed what the director or the other actors expected of him. He's never added an "uh" or a comma—he's impeccable—100% what I wrote, not a breath more. I don't work with actors where 90% is yours and 10% is theirs—I just wouldn't tolerate that. Nathan doesn't do it just for me—he does it for Neil Simon or John Guare. He said the only music the actor has to work with is what the playwright gave him, so he said, why would I start adding? My character's in the words and not in extraneous stuff. Which is exactly the way Callas felt about music—it's in the notes Bellini, Verdi, Rossini wrote, so don't fuck around with it. The truth is there, and you bring what you can.

TZ: Your career has been closely associated with the Manhattan Theatre Club; how has that affiliation affected your work?

TMcN: Well, my first play was done when I was twenty-three; now I'm fifty-six. That's a lot of years. I've had several careers. My first play—done on Broadway—what a phenomenon, a disaster with the critics, then the Off-Broadway years, then *Broadway, Broadway* closed in Philadelphia, then regrouping, beginning again with Manhattan Theatre Club—I did *Bad Habits* with them way up on 74th Street. So I'm on my fourth career, now. I'll always be very proud of *Where Has Tommy Flowers Gone?*, and I'm very proud of *The Ritz.*

With the Manhattan Theatre Club, I consider myself as fortunate as any playwright who's ever lived. They made such a commitment to me—they don't make me compete with myself, and they've gone out a limb for me so many times. A lot of my plays have been successful, but that last one, *Ganesh*, was not as successful as *Lips Together*. Another theatre would have said, let's do a workshop of *Love! Valour! Compassion!*, let's make sure we have a hit this time, but they don't do that to me, and I can't tell you the freedom.

I'm not like that hypothetical writer who's trying to write a play that he or she *thinks* the theatre wants to produce, I'm writing what I want to write, and I'm pleased when other people like it. But Lynne Meadow [Artistic Director of Manhattan Theatre Club] isn't making me feel I owe them a hit. So many people say they're committed to a writer, but what they really are is committed to a writer of a successful play, and when they read the next play, and they don't think it's going to be as successful as the last one, they say, well, we'll take a raincheck. I think it's amazing that this play was as successful as it was—when I turned it in, I don't think Lynne thought for one second that this play was going to be this kind of success. I'm sure that if you answer those matchbook cover ads, "Learn to Be a Writer," they tell you "be true to yourself," and so often we aren't. When I wrote *Frankie and Johnny*, I thought it would never be produced, but Lynne said she'd produce anything I wrote, and we did it in a workshop, then in a small theatre, then in a big theatre. Each time I thought, well, it'll stop here, and it went on to become a movie. I thought, it's of interest to people who have just turned forty—wouldn't interest an older audience, wouldn't interest a younger audience, and. . . .

I've never written a play that is actively hostile to an audience, which if you're really angry is a temptation. I can't talk about my development as a writer without talking about the Manhattan Theatre Club—without that theatre, I wouldn't be here—I can't imagine my life. During the preview of *It's Only a Play*, which is sort of how I hooked up with that theatre, Lynne said: I'll produce your next play sight unseen. It was a few days before Christmas, and it was the greatest Christmas gift I've ever gotten. In a funny way I didn't quite believe her—I couldn't believe it—but she meant it, and she's meant it ever since.

It's a great responsibility, but I keep saying to myself, write what you want to write and be truthful and people may not like it but they'll respond at some level. When it gets dishonest, then. . . . The Manhattan Theatre Club has an older audience—average age is about sixty, and they tend to be fairly conservative, and I say to myself, Oh, I better not do this. Then I say, no, write the play, they will survive it or they'll walk out, but it's not going to kill anybody and you're not going to close the theatre. It's not as though you raised $4 million for Broadway. Even if this [*Love! Valour! Compassion!*] had been the biggest flop in their history, they'd still be opening the next show [since it's a subscription season]. So I don't say to myself, "I owe it to Lynne"—she never said that, that's you. So I'm so grateful to them.

I think of myself as someone trying to earn a living as a playwright, and my friends as people trying to earn their livings as playwrights—that's a challenge, and it's hard, and I think I've been lucky and I've persevered. This is my life, right here in this building [Manhattan Theatre Club]—they've done eight plays of mine in ten years. The commitment has to be to the writer—anybody would have produced *Streetcar Named Desire*—where were the producers at the end of his life for *Ville Carre*? Every writer has valleys—nobody goes from masterpiece to masterpiece. Shakespeare did not go from *Hamlet* to *Lear* to *The Tempest*.

TZ: *Love! Valour! Compassion!* has generated a good bit of critical controversy—both in and out of the gay community, from both the conservative Right and the Queer Left—about your treatment of these characters. How does it fit into the history of gay drama?

TMcN: That's hard to answer. I didn't out of the blue write the first gay play—there was *Boys in the Band*. But historically? That's for other people to answer. My very first play, *And Things That Go Bump in the Night,* had gay characters in it, but the big difference was that was really a shocking play in its day, and I don't think *Love! Valour! Compassion!* is particularly shocking. People discuss the nudity in it, but what I'm really proud of is that everyone has tolerated and accepted an enormous amount of affection and tenderness between men. The most common comment I get is that by the end of Act One, they forget they're gay men and just think of them as human beings they can identify with, and I take that as a compliment. They are specifically these eight gay men, but they're individual people; I didn't write them as generic types. Everyone identifies with one or two or maybe even all of them. People say I was moved by these people; I wasn't threatened by them; I wasn't harangued by them; I wasn't intimidated by them; they didn't seem so exotic to me—I know these people. There's a humanity going back and forth between the actors and the audience—you can feel it in the theatre.

TZ: Are other art forms, besides music, an influence on your work? The set design of *Love! Valour! Compassion!* seemed to me very painterly, the last scene especially, much like an Eakins.

TMcN: Both dance and music make me feel inarticulate—they do things that I think playwriting can't. Dance is very important to me. I think dance is the best way of depicting love, physical, sensual love between people. Certainly I think that's hardest to convey in theatre. Love is expressed fabulously in dance—I think sexual passion is expressed better in dance than in words. Dance is about transitions—in theatre that's the hardest thing—so you go to the ballet and outside the theatre are these wonderful ballet photos, and they are not poses, but they are moments in time. How did they get there? Baryshnikov was not born six feet in the air. That's all about transitions. Going to the dance has made me freer as a writer in many ways. There's a freedom in dance that I'm trying to find in my writing. The transition between comedy and the serious—if anything I pride myself on doing it's those transitions which some critics have faulted me for—that's how I see life. It's like last night—I was walking along a street, and I fell down an unseen incline and ripped the most expensive suit I ever bought in my life. No one prepared me: get ready, you're about to fall on your ass.

I go to museums a lot—I get to the Met[ropolitan Museum of Art] or the Modern at least once a month. It's important to have kindred people who are trying to talk about the same things you're talking about. So you can say to a designer, it's sort of like Matisse here, or to talk about music and say, it's the sort of a moment that reminds me of. . . . It's nice to know that you're not alone.

I still go to the theatre I bet three times a week—and that's over fifty-two weeks a year—so I bet I see a hundred and fifty plays a year, and the other four nights are divided between ballet and opera. I think it's so important to see what's going on in other arts.

I've never been bored for a moment of my life in New York—I've been bored almost every other place but never in New York. I had my bags packed to move to New York from age twelve. I went from my high school graduation to the Trailways bus terminal, but I thought I was going to be a journalist. Operas were something you could see if you lived in a big city. Plays were really the last component of all this for me.

TZ: Shakespeare comes up in your plays as well as your conversation so often. Would you talk about that influence?

TMcN: He's the most obvious influence. Every play of his has a different sound world, a different texture to it—that is such genius—the poetry, the language, the sounds of *Othello* are different from the sounds of *Lear* are different from the sounds of *Twelfth Night*. That's a goal to aspire to. As you get older, you come to appreciate the non-judgmental quality in Shakespeare's writing. When I think of my earlier work, it's much more judgmental, writing your opinions of characters—these are good people, these are bad people—Shakespeare just writes the people. I love the democracy of his plays which I have never really attained in mine. You can't write a Shakespearean play— if I were a composer I'd want to be influenced by Mozart—a role model. His daring to say "Never never never never never"—everything to be learned about playwriting can be learned from that one moment. Shakespeare is the original show-biz kid: let's put a show on! He's not a poet dreaming in a garret but a very practical man with a lot of competition.

I had a wonderful high school English teacher and a professor at Columbia who taught us Shakespeare's thirty-six plays chronologically, so I have a sense of the playwright's career. He followed *Hamlet* with *Measure for Measure*—you don't jump. That's what I meant about transitions—what can a playwright learn from ballet? Ballet is all about transitions. You don't just write a great scene, you have to get there—how do you get them on stage? How do you get them off? I had a really old-fashioned education and I'm so grateful for that now.

TZ: Your plays are often called Chekhovian. Is Chekhov a conscious influence?

TMcN: I'm not as interested in plot as I used to be, or in the social issues of the day. When I was in college I thought *Wild Duck* was better than anything in Chekhov, but now I've come to appreciate Chekhov. With *And Things That Go Bump in the Night*, sections of it were influenced by Albee, but after that I found my own voice. Chekhov is an influence, Beckett is an influence, but I don't write like them.

I don't get the logic of imitation. When I teach playwriting, whoever's been the hit of the season, that's who everybody writes like—Mamet, Durang, Wasserstein. But this is what I try not to think about when I'm writing—I try to keep it to "He says, She says." If I started to worry about my style, I'd dry up. It's occurred to me over the past few years that I'm not interested in the overview;

what I'm interested in is the small moment—I think there's enormous drama in that.

I think I have an instinct to tell a story in space and time, not narratively; I'm not a novelist *manqué*. It's a natural inclination—the only formal training I had in playwriting was sitting in the last row of the second balcony.

Chapter Two
The Early Plays of Terrence McNally

Howard Stein

I

And Things That Go Bump in the Night, a family play, was written as a one-act play in the summer of 1962 and called at that time, *There Is Something Out There*. McNally was twenty-three years old. He inherited a theater tradition inundated with family plays. From 1920 to 1960, the American Theater was especially populated with plays that concentrated on family relationships, among the most famous being *Desire Under the Elms*, *The Silver Cord*, *Street Scene*, *Holiday*, *Awake and Sing!*, *The Little Foxes*, *Our Town*, *The Glass Menagerie*, *All My Sons*, *Death of a Salesman*, *The Dark at the Top of the Stairs*, *A Raisin in the Sun*. Some of these plays dealt with social issues in addition to the domestic ones; nevertheless, the plays centered on the battles between parents and children, exploitation of the generation gap, confrontations between and among siblings, and the rigors of growing up. Frequently the parents were villainous, treated somewhat unsympathetically by the playwright who was usually at the very beginning of his career. Youth was most frequently seen as more knowledgeable, more honest, more admirable, and more aware than the parents. The results: the kids taught the parents how to live, how to face reality, and how to face their own hypocrisy. While the children were preparing to run off to catch the freedom train, the parents were left behind either to suffer a self-inflicted death or an isolation they so richly deserved. In their rebellious yearning for liberty, the young unmask the older generation, punish them, battle with the values of their elders, and finally abandon them.

The scenes were familiar: sons and daughters trying to spread their wings and fly into the great blue yonder, parents trying to fulfill their responsibilities by putting limits on children's anarchic spirits in an attempt to direct them to a positive future, children mistaking authority for tyranny, parents mistaking youthful exuberance and natural rebellion for disrespect and ignorance. The generation gap is posited on the following principles from the parent's point of view: youth can learn from maturity, but they won't; youth need not repeat the mistakes of the parents, but they do. From the children's point of view: the parents are at the mercy of lies and deceit as well as hypocrisy; parents have lost their energy to explore and seek experience, demanding that their twenty-year-old children think as if they were forty; parents have accepted patterns and systems that are not to the benefit of the youth, who, therefore, wants to alter, destroy and replace. In *Street Scene*, Sam and Rose leave their neighborhood and what is left of their families in order to go out and make a better world. Alexandra, Regina's daughter in *The Little Foxes*, leaves a corrupt New Orleans household and abandons her mother in order to discover another geography in which the foxes have been replaced by more human creatures. Biff in *Death of a Salesman* leaves the Loman home in Brooklyn in search of his own identity in Texas. Tom in *The Glass Menagerie* leaves behind in St. Louis his heart and his conscience but holds on to his vision and private yearnings while exploring the high seas. Linda in *Holiday* leaves a value system that provides her with no moral and emotional gratification and runs off with Johnny against her father's demands and her sister's wishes because she seeks to discover her own fingerprints.

In these plays, the playwright usually establishes one dominant parent: Regina in *The Little Foxes*, Mrs. Phelps in *The Silver Cord*, Mr. Eaton in *Holiday*, Bessie in *Awake and Sing!*, Willy in *Death of a Salesman*, Amanda in *The Glass Menagerie*, Ephraim in *Desire Under the Elms*, Ruth in *A Raisin in the Sun*. Frequently the playwright will choose a family in which the dead parent haunts the living household. However this is accomplished, the playwright still manages to have the children teach the adults. (Notice how this pattern continues into the seventies and the eighties in plays such as *Sticks and Bones* by David Rabe, *Buried Child* by Sam Shepard, *Equus* by Peter Shaffer, *'night Mother* by Marsha Norman.)

In these plays, except in the case of O'Neill's dramas, the dramatic event never soars above the domestic, social, or psychological reality and never leaves the audience confused or bewildered. The "message" is frequently stated point blank: "life should not be written on dollar bills"; "blow out your candles, Laura, for the world is lit by lightning"; "attention must be paid"; "Mama, just for a moment . . . let's look at one another . . . that's all human beings are, just blind people." The characters are recognizable if not altogether familiar, completely accessible to the audience, whose language is, for the most part, the language of the people in the play. The audience shares the habits and the values that they recognize as crucial to the drama even if their lives are not identical to the lives of the players. The people in the play have conflicts, but their behavior to one another is in the realm of civility; they have significant differences but somehow have the well-being of the adversary in their consciousness. They have good manners, and their self-interest is modified by an honorable other-interest. They may exercise a little irony but very little, a little criticism but very little, be guilty of a temper tantrum but one which can be forgiven in the context. These people are struggling with their human predicament; most of them have their hearts and minds in the right place even if their intelligence is circumscribed by age and circumstance. These are good people who might take a bad direction. Audiences could understand if not forgive, sympathize if not approve, acknowledge if not applaud. It was all human, understandable, and all too common. Most important, the presentation was familiar.

Not so with Terrence McNally in 1962. His family play is surreal rather than realistic, his concerns metaphysical rather than the physical and the commonplace, his treatment more savage than civil, more nasty than ironic, more fierce than compassionate, and more confusing than clear. Instead of a living room or a parlor or a dining room, familiar settings for the family dramas of the first half of this century (bedrooms were for farce only!), McNally offers the following description of the setting for his play:

At rise the stage is empty. Absolute silence. Pitch dark. After a moment the red light on top of the intercom goes on and we begin to hear the terrible grunting and groaning noises of a person just waking up from a long and deep sleep. The sounds must be amplified to an almost unendurable volume. The theater should reverberate. We hear a bed table

laden with medicine bottles and knickknacks crashing to the floor. And
then, after a yawn of agonizing dimensions, we hear:

Ruby's Voice (A pronouncement): I'm awake. The Ruby is awake. Buon
    giorno a tutti! (11)

We soon discover that the scene-setting is a basement. Later
Clarence, the guest for the night, says, "That's what's so wonderful
about it. It doesn't look at all like a basement. It's so . . . so cheerful."
(43) Grandfa responds in the manner of the household in answer to
Clarence's civility, politeness, intelligent hypocrisy: "Well, we tried
to brighten it up some. A little blood, a little spleen" (43).

And Things That Go Bump in the Night was finished in 1963
and first produced professionally in 1964, two years after *Who's Afraid*
of Virginia Woolf? Before the new wave of McNally, Albee, Kopit,
and Richardson, audiences were comfortable with traditional expectations. However, to receive this play, not necessarily to like it or
approve of it, but simply to receive it, we must enter the world
McNally has created; he has not entered ours. And therein lies the
theatrical revolution.

This play's family lives in a basement protected by an electric
fence which electrocutes animals and human beings who get too
close. The family is made up of Grandfa (he is about to go off to
some old persons' home when "they" finally come to get him); Fa
(Ruby's husband, very, very quiet and subordinate, who seems to
sleep all day as well as all night with intermittent moments of consciousness); Sigfrid (twenty-one, the son whom Ruby appropriates
as her accomplice, disciple, and errand boy); Lakme (thirteen-year-
old daughter, uncertain about her mother and brother and their "vo-
cation," in conflict with her brother and intimidated by her mother),
Clarence (the evening's victim/guest), and Ruby (the matriarch who
sleeps all day in preparation for the nightly escapade of killing a
guest, a paragon of evil with a sarcastic, malicious tongue to match
her actions). The action of the play has everything to do with the
bumps in the night, but the bumps are never alluded to in the drama
nor are they heard until the final moments of the play. The only
reference is on the title page just below the title where McNally posts
an epigraph:

From ghoulies and ghosts
Long leggitie beasties
And things that go bump in the night
Good Lord deliver us!

—*fourteenth-century Scottish Folk Prayer*

Each night the household offers a victim to the "Good Lord" who is sacrificially electrocuted on the fence that protects the underground refuge. Act I gets the family ready for the guest over the protestation of Grandfa and the questioning of Lakme. The victim has been recruited in town that day by Sigfrid, who discovered an old school chum named Clarence, whom he has invited to join the family for the evening. Clarence makes his entrance at the end of Act I. Act II is devoted to his demise. That encounter which makes the drama of Act II is driven by Ruby who humiliates and challenges Clarence and by Sigfrid's revelation of a homoerotic encounter between himself and Clarence. This encounter eventually sends Clarence into a frenzy which catapults him out of the basement into the electric fence and his death. Grandfa battles for the soul of Sigfrid but loses to an invincible Ruby, and bumps begin to thump as Ruby's final monologue closes the play.

They teach Clarence that the way he lives deserves contempt and ridicule: "The way I live is . . . the best I can do. [. . .] I think I am becoming a better human being day by day. [. . .] Anything that makes you want to live so bad . . . you'd die for it . . . Shakespeare, Florence . . . someone in the park. That's what I believe in." (59–60). Clarence finally explodes in a burst of fire, the victim of Ruby and her allies. The image of the murdered Clarence remains, as Ruby's hysterical laughter together with Clarence's recorded voice, "ever and forever and forever. I don't want to ever go home" (74) provides a shattering conclusion. If Clarence's "The way I live" is without value to the Rubys of this world, what *is* the way to live?

McNally was not the first in this theatrical revolution, but he was certainly in the vanguard. The very early plays of Edward Albee, *The American Dream, Sandbox,* and especially *The Zoo Story* seem to have had an immediate influence. This assumption is predicated on the sound of the plays and the tone of the drama: the slashing sarcasm, the biting sardonic dialogue, the baiting of one character by another as a form of aggression and cruelty, the rage expressed by Ruby in her relentless drive to gain her objective, the bitter exchanges between family members. Clarence articulates our feeling as a stranger in that household:

I don't know what to think of you people. One minute you're friendly, the next you're making fun of me. (57)

Sigfrid can only mouth to Grandfa, "I love you," because he can't bring himself to say it aloud. For it is hate and fury that provide the energy for the people in the play, not unlike the qualities that seem to drive Jerry in *The Zoo Story* and Martha in *Who's Afraid of Virginia Woolf?* In this latter play, Albee titles the first act "Get the Guests." McNally "gets the guest" as well. However, while Albee's guests are hurt, brutalized, and finally dispatched to a life that has been temporarily shattered, McNally's guest is killed. Sigfrid remains behind, choosing not to abandon his parents nor his sister:

Ruby: Sigfrid. What will become of us?
Sigfrid: (after a moment): Nothing.
Ruby: No?
Sigfrid: We will continue (And again the thump from outside.) (89)

This play is not about young people trying to make their way in the world without the controlling factor of parents; it is not about youthful impulses against mature judgments; it is not about parents trying to help the children understand life, nor is it about parents trying to save, to protect, and to serve their young. This play has no message. Still, it has elements common to those traditional family plays. Like those plays, it also has two children, a weak parent (who is present but absent), a dominant parent of tyrannical force, and conflict among family members seeking their own identity. But unlike those earlier plays, this play is an emotional journey that should lead the reader or the audience to a deeply felt awareness of suppressed evil—not disagreement, not dissension—but evil.

Such an awareness was the function of the earliest drama that we know in Western dramatic literature, but we have left behind such drama for the easier, accessible, comfortable drama of realism.

The emotional journey in the traditional American family plays is very easy, very recognizable, very comfortable in that we know what we are seeing is directed to our conscious selves. In the traditional American family plays, we the audience go through an experience that might or could happen to any of us. However in the ancient theater 2500 years ago, anything could happen in that space and anything should happen in that space. That space is the theater-reality, not life-reality. In that theater we can be exposed to what is strange, unfamiliar, wild, frightening and threatening, where what is presented attempts to touch us not where we live in our daily lives but where secrets and mysteries and dangerous impulses linger and hover beneath the stuff of those daily lives. The stage is a place where a stepmother can lust for a stepson, where a son can murder his mother who has already murdered his father, where a son can kill his father and bed his mother, where a mother can encourage her son to bring home a guest as a sacrificial lamb. In the best of theater, the audience is forced to endure the activation of repressed desires, not just conscious desires or even suppressed desires as traditional American family plays would have it. The audience in the theater would be forced to entertain impulses that they have not only denied but ignored, a healing process, which is the quality of experience that McNally offers us in *And Things That Go Bump in the Night*.

A mysterious force of some sort is announced at the very beginning of the play:

Fa: It's moving west . . . the government says it's moving west.
Grandfa: What is? What's moving west?
Fa: It. (12)

The "it" resonates with associations to the hydrogen and atomic bombs, just as the basement, the shelter, resonates with associations; as Fa says, "No one's gonna die down here, not in our sanctuary." At the time of the writing of this play, the nation was preoccupied with bomb shelters, and although Ruby's clan never mentions nuclear weapons, the audience is allowed to make its own associations. The play is of its own time while it faces the questions of all times.

McNally mentions that "the play is about fear and negation" (7), and Ruby, its heroine, acts out a nihilistic vision which is her answer to "The Way We Live." Despair hovers over the play like smothering parents. No social, political, domestic, or national issue is significant with respect to the issue of how we live. Ruby has lost any reason to be: no faith, no hope, no charity. She is left with an action: "And if we are without charity, we suckle from the bitter root of its absence . . . wherefrom we shall draw the sustenance to destroy you" (90)

The play is a shocker, not just because of its courage and its drive to the edge and over but because it also contains the strands of those old domestic and social conditions: child rebellion, parental obligations and responsibilities, the hope for the future, sibling rivalry. (One of the most significant subjects that is totally absent, is the subject of money. In American plays in general and in American family plays in particular, money has always been a major consideration.)

Ruby is alive with her despair and her ability to draw sustenance from the absence of charity. The spectacular nature of Ruby, her passionate yearning to destroy, hurt, and hate makes her a black saint, as complete as a Genet character, as narrow, as single-minded, and as unyielding, a startling creation for a twenty-three-year-old American playwright. Whatever flaws the readers find in this play, whatever limits they conclude about the kind of drama or the kind of theater available to them with this play, the fact remains that *And Things That Go Bump in the Night* is something original, outrageous, and audacious, the product of a genuine creative talent. Nurtured on hate and disgust rather than love and compassion or tea and sympathy, *And Things That Go Bump in the Night* is far ahead of those old-fashioned domestic dramas in providing us with an insight and experience into the genuine nature of the human condition.

Prosaic talent engages us in tales that help deal with generational problems, marriage problems, economic problems, educational problems, domestic problems. But poetic talent is always preoccupied with the problems of living and dying, of loving and losing. The prosaic problems tend to overwhelm our daily lives so that the poetic problems are seldom if ever confronted. The young Terrence McNally offers us a genuine confrontation: no answer, only a confrontation.

II

McNally's next long play, *Where Has Tommy Flowers Gone?*, was produced at the Yale Repertory Theater in January 1971. Between these two long plays, he wrote and produced a number of short pieces. Although these shorter plays were not as ambitious as the longer ones, they shared the same sardonic tone, satiric edge and ironic treatment, but they were not nearly so outrageous as *And Things That Go Bump in the Night*.

During this first decade of McNally's output, the theater in America was producing for the first time in its history a concentrated group of plays that were critical of the U.S. government, that were examining the roots of corruption in the nation, that were devoted to the political and historical concerns that formed the development of this country. Not only were the nation's blemishes exposed (as they were in *Streetcar*, *Death of a Salesman*, *Awake and Sing!*, *The Little Foxes*, et al.), but more significantly the sins of omission and commission, the immorality, the poison which was now manifest in what came to be called "a sick society" was on view. Consider: *1776*, *1492*, *America Hurrah*, *US*, *God Bless*, *Indians*, *Macbird*, *Blues for Mr. Charlie*, *The Old Glory*, *We Bombed in New Haven*, *The Great White Hope*, *Viet Rock*. Never in the history of the theater in this country had so many plays making political and cultural indictments been presented to the general public. The nation was obliged to examine its own heritage and behavior.

The success of these plays was in great part a result of each play's choosing a specific target to attack in its satiric blast. McNally, on the other hand, tended to be more general than specific in his attacks, and his plays could be described as "extended anecdotes . . . [which] hazard broad satire" (Cohn, 19–20). These shorter pieces, even *Tommy Flowers*, are essentially inoffensive. They touch politics and society, even comment in their own way with a degree of effectiveness, but in the final analysis, their effect is more in the realm of commentary and entertainment than offense or assault.

Bringing It All back Home contains echoes of Albee's *The American Dream* and David Rabe's *Sticks and Bones* and is the only one of these short pieces that is specifically a family play although it focuses on issues connected to the Vietnam war. The "It" of the title has a number of possible referents. The first is to Jimmy, the older son

who, like David in *Sticks and Bones*, has been brought back home
from Vietnam. But where David in Rabe's play is returned home
blind and psychologically tormented, Jimmy in McNally's play is
sent home dead. He has been brought home in a crate, suggesting
that he is an "It" rather than a human being, carried home as an "It"
rather than in a humanizing casket. As the family moves through
their routines, the "It" soon seems to refer to "how we live," to family values, to all those cultural forces that define that family. The "It"
might refer to the catastrophic political decision by the U.S. to go to
war in Vietnam. The "It" also echoes "making it," an American cliché
that resonates with the fundamental values of our nation. All these
possibilities add to the implications of the play, but in the final analysis, McNally seems most concerned with the American family, its
values and its preoccupations, the mother with her hair dryer, the
children with their sexual escapades and with their concern for money,
and the father with his hidden sexual yearnings and adventures. The
question raised in such an environment is, what did Jimmy die for?
The answer seems to be the perpetuation of such emptiness:

*Mother: Right or wrong, Jimmy gave his life for his country and if that's
not the American way of doing things, I'd like to know what is. (20)*

The description of the setting at the outset of the play separates
this play from the earlier bizarre family play, *And Things That Go
Bump in the Night*:

*A living room. Comfortably furnished, nice proportions. Front door,
door leading off to kitchen, stairs leading up. (3)*

A perfect setting for a satire on the American home, 1968, but a far
cry from the eccentric savage attack in the earlier play. Nevertheless,
there are some similarities. The children duel with each other in
much the way that Sigfrid and Lakme do. Like Grandfa in *And Things
That Go Bump in the Night*, this play has a character with something
of a conscience, Miss Horne, a television reporter who attempts to
dispel the romantic and fanciful notions of the family. She has come
to film the homecoming of Jimmy while the family prepares for its
fifteen minutes of fame. She is sarcastic, mocking, insulting, and

disgusted with them, sufficiently so as to have the father return from his fantasies and his homophobia to warn the public: "I want you the people out there to know this is a Negro who is saying all this . . . a black troublemaker" (21).

The play's tone, on the other hand, is not unlike that tone established earlier by McNally. When Jimmy is delivered in a crate, Son calls Mother:

Son: (Goes to door, opens it, admits two men carrying large box who
    bring it to the center of the room.) Mom! It's Jimmy!
Mother: (off) I'm in the dryer.(7)

Jimmy, who frequently rises from the dead to address the audience, responds to her scream of "JIIIMMMMMYYYY" with, "Then do us all a favor, don't watch the evening news" (22).

Like *And Things That Go Bump in the Night*, the play takes the reader on an emotional journey, but this trip does not attack the underside of the reader, does not force the reader or the audience to grapple with the evil deeds and doings of Ruby and Sigfrid, does not grapple with the ultimate question of "To be or not to be," but instead merely observes how we do live in this country. It attacks our conscious values and concerns, and on that level offers the reader or the audience satire that is ironic, funny, bizarre, and touching. The cartoon characters raise their progeny and suffer or ignore their fate in ignorance. Jimmy (It) is brought home to conclude that the main reason he wishes he was alive is so he could figure out why he was dead. With broad strokes, McNally paints a picture of contemporary America—an indictment of a senseless war as well as of materialistic and artificial values in the nation's homes, issues worthy of a more particular, specific targeting.

Four of the remaining six short early plays deal either directly or indirectly with war, Vietnam, or political policy. *Botticelli* takes place on the battlefield in Vietnam; *Next*, in the U.S. Army recruiting offices; *¡Cuba Si!* is set in Central Park despite its preoccupation with the Cuban revolution, and *Witness* evokes the assassination of President Kennedy.

Botticelli is a mild, political attack on the senseless and inhuman war in Vietnam. In its condemnation, it is schematically amusing. Two soldiers are playing a game while they wait with their weapons poised for a Vietcong soldier to come out of his tunnel. Unable to solve the riddle which is their game, "Name a dead European male in the arts beginning with a 'P'," they kill the enemy while unsuccessfully offering names as a solution to their riddle. After the murder of the victim, while the spotlight remains on the dead soldier, they continue guessing the answer, finally solving the puzzle with a contemporary of Botticelli; the loser of the game says, "Never heard of him," as they had never heard of Vietnam nor their dead adversary. The play is an exercise in McNally's virtuosity as a playwright and reflects his considerable ability as a satirist, but the target is again neither sufficiently sharp nor compelling.

The target in *Next* is the army recruiting institution for a war that is not just unpopular but unreasonable. Marion Cheever, a fat man in his late forties, has come for his physical. He is frightened, outraged, and resentful, and the ensuing examination contains all the conventional expectations in that situation. None of his protests has an effect on his examiner; none of his explanations interferes with the evaluation of his physical condition. The play provides a vehicle for the actor performing Marion, who becomes more and more desperate in a situation which is devoid of reason. And at the end of his examination, there is the "next" inductee. The play never veers from the scene and situation, demonstrating McNally's fertility in inventing moments for the actor. The final invention is the most dramatic; Cheever turns the tables on his examiner, Sgt. Thech, forcing the officer to do as Cheever demands, ultimately writing down everything Cheever dictates, including the final fact that he is indeed unacceptable on his terms not the army's. The play is entertaining and critical but more amusing than subversive.

The political target is clearest in *¡Cuba Si!,* in which a Cuban female guerrilla named Cuba has established a beachhead in Central Park on a mission given her by Fidel Castro: ". . . vaya a los Estados Unidos, and make the revolution. . . . *They* make the Bay of Pigs; *we* make the Bay of Pigs" (85). The subject here is clearly the U.S. political policy toward Cuba, an adversarial policy based upon fear of that island's future plans for communism in the Western Hemisphere. A liberal reporter from the *New York Times* has come to interview the revolutionary while she is fighting off the "spy bitches." The interview culminates with Cuba's insistence that the revolution will succeed in the U.S., while the reporter claims America is immune to revolution and thus another target rears its head: American complacency, this issue is raised only at the end of the play.

In 1963 our newspapers were filled with CIA gossip about attempts to assassinate Castro and about U.S. insistence that the communist regime be overthrown. McNally uses his satiric talent to invent the revolutionary Cuba and to provide the character with such color, energy, and charm that any actress would yearn to portray that figure. At the same time we can see McNally's tongue in his cheek:

Cuba: Bastard! Hooligan bastard. (volley of shots). . . . How do you like those apples, Mr. CIA?
Voice: (Offstage) I'm dying, Cuba! (85)

The allusion to *Antony and Cleopatra* is clear. But McNally's cleverness undercuts the play. The revolutionary fervor so energizing the United States of America in 1968 is dissipated with wit. Cuba's mission in the U.S. is doomed, and that doom is offered as an indictment of the placid, uninvolved, unreflecting and uncaring population described by Cuba earlier in the interview with the reporter.

Cuba: . . . Cuba has seen your city: it stinks. Your politicians: they stink. Your social programs: they stink. Your newspapers: they stink. Your public transportation: it stinks. Your architecture: it stinks. Your leader: he stinks. Your leader's lady: she stinks. A reporter: you stink. Only one thing does not stink: your young people. (Pause) Why you say not everyone in the world care about the revolution? (91)

The statement is a very sixties message: the nation stinks in every way except for its youth, which yearns for a revolution. But what revolution? A communist uprising like that in Cuba? An economic revolution rather than a communistic one? A social revolution? A revolution of arson with the burning of the United States in order to start all over again? The play offers nothing more than the youth promoting revolution in 1968 did. But it does offer the spirit of rebellion prevalent in 1968 United States and the passion for change, a spirit we will see more of in *Where Has Tommy Flowers Gone?* three years later. Still, when the reporter tells her that "Cuba is for Cubans and you're a helluva long way off base as far as anyone in the big leagues is concerned . . . that stuff you preach, it won't make any headway here" (95), the play ends with Cuba smiling as the thunder roars and the lightning strikes. What indeed is the fate of the U.S.? The play stirs some genuine emotions and attitudes in the American soul in 1996 as well as in 1968.

Witness and *Sweet Eros* share the same dramatic invention: a person is abducted, tied to a chair, and harangued by either one person or a group of people for the length of the play—a captive audience. *Witness*, however, moves beyond the abduction or kidnapping in order to deal with the implications of presidential assassination, the locale of the play being reminiscent of the Book Depository in Dallas from which President Kennedy was shot. The decade was rampant with assassination—Malcolm X, Martin Luther King, Robert Kennedy—and murder of major figures was cheap. "Off the cops" was not just a slogan. The nation began to behave as if the solution to its problems was murder.

The victim in *Witness* is to be a witness to yet another assassination of an American president, an action that seems to emanate from an ill-informed, anarchic, distorted mind, one that believes such an act will cure what ails the nation. While waiting for the presidential caravan in order to strike the fatal blow, the play gives us, for the first time in the McNally canon, the theme of loneliness, individual loneliness, as a major subject. A variety of people pass through the room where the witness remains a prisoner and each tells his lonely story. The kidnapper, angry and bitter, binds and gags his prisoner and then reads a letter from Holden Caulfield—of *The Catcher in the Rye*—which articulates his feelings, not just the diatribe against phoniness for which Holden is famous but about his failure to find any way other than killing the president in order to do something constructive for his nation. Most of us have forgotten that Holden's objective in life was to be the catcher in the rye, to stand at the edge of the field of rye and keep people from falling over the edge, a heroic idea appropriate to youth and idealists. The gunshots at the end come "from every window for blocks and blocks" (137), indicating that the entire country is packed with lonely, frustrated, and violent people. The play closes with the audience knowing that something is rotten in the state of the union.

Unlike *Witness*, *Sweet Eros* is about love and sex. Again a victim is kidnapped, again bound and gagged. In this play, the victim is harangued by the abductor, who has both loved too much and been betrayed by the object of his love and loved too little and caused his beloved to commit suicide. The victim never speaks but later in the play sings while attempting to free herself. In the final scene we see them in a condition of co-existence, a sort of sweet eros without the dynamics and frustrations that come with pure eros, an antidote to the loneliness felt both in love and out of love.

The pattern in American playwriting is that the first play is a family play; the second play is a sex play, and then the playwright goes on to explore world and universal concerns. *Noon* was McNally's second appearance on Broadway, while all the other short pieces were introduced Off-Broadway and Off-Off Broadway. This play is his sex play as *And Things That Go Bump in the Night* was his family play. *Noon* is only about sex: homosexual, heterosexual, and orgysexual, a sitcom activated by a newspaper item suggesting and encouraging liaisons and adventures. Mistaken identities, mistaken expectations, mistaken satisfactions all compete to offer a commercially-oriented audience titters, asides, muffled laughter, and uninhibited guffaws. No one gets harmed; no one gets satisfaction; no one departs outraged, nor does anyone depart one bit wiser from this amusing, cute, accessible short piece that was sandwiched in between "Morning" and "Night" for the Broadway presentation of *Morning, Noon, and Night*.

III

Where Has Tommy Flowers Gone? is a series of episodes in which Tommy, the prototypical sixties flower child, goes on a freedom ride in which he engages in a spectacular number of spontaneous adventures. His anarchic spirit, his American ingenuity, his endless resourcefulness, and imaginative inventions provide him with the muscle, the energy, the talent to go from one wild experience to the next, during which time he is totally irresponsible in the sense that middle-class morality would have it. Tommy is a spirit of total freedom, an anarchic temperament that seeks satisfaction, self-satisfaction, no matter what the restraint.

In the opening monologue of the play, Tommy addresses the audience with a speech that he offers to account for his personality and character:

Tommy: I would like to thank the following people for making me what I am today. (9)

And he spends more than three hundred words thanking individuals and institutions. The fact is that Tommy Flowers is a product. He is what others have made him. The Flower Generation, which could not trust anyone over thirty (at the opening of the play Tommy is thirty), assumed its righteous character as contrast to the corrupt character of their elders. Tommy, like the flower children, looks upon himself as pure, a child who does not need to grow up. By bringing to bear the fact that he is not only essentially but also actually a product of forces outside of himself, he establishes himself as a victim of the system, of the society, of being born in St. Petersburg, of having middle-class conventional parents, of having to find money in order to survive. He exists and flourishes on his charm (of which he has an abundance), his wits (which have more to do with strategic entrepreneurship than with intelligence) and his power as an actor. Tommy can imitate stars of either gender, a first-class passenger on an airline, his own mother—the list is endless and provides abundant entertainment. The actor chosen to portray Tommy Flowers has a field day.

Harold Clurman paints this portrait of Tommy:

. . . he neither learns nor protests, he does not yearn or despair. In a word, he is not a true person. He is a peg on which to hang all the clichés about our shabby time. No community whatsoever would make Tommy anything other than what he is, because he is a lump incapable of the volition needed for good or evil, the human material to develop toward meaningful purity or damnable baseness. (799)

The nation's shabby values are spiritually inhibiting, and despite Clurman's accurate picture of Tommy, one can nevertheless discover in the character of Tommy Flowers youthful arrogance, fire, energy, and creativity—qualities that are the envy of anyone caught up in the daily struggle with the shabby values.

Soon after the opening monologue in which Tommy claims he is what the society has made him, he tells Gerta that he is "a summa cum something from somewhere in my head, no prospects in mind and lots of bridges burned behind me, an honorable discharge from Uncle Sam . . ."(15). Tommy is always "putting everyone on," as they said in the sixties. One lie or truth is as good as another, for the only thing that counts is that Tommy is entertaining, charismatic, amusing, and delightful. The cast of characters include Gerta, an airline hostess who is a perfect foil for Tommy's jokes and wit; Arnold, a silent dog who is Tommy's devoted friend; Ben Delight, an actor who accompanies Tommy and provides us with the chance to meet an entertaining cab driver in a trip to Bloomingdale's that is pure Aristophanic farce; Nedda, who becomes Tommy's love life until he abandons her with the check in the restaurant and then tries to re-capture her from the street while she is incarcerated in the Women's House of Detention. The series of episodes is hilarious, but they are only situations, events, happenings, contributing to a lively display of the playwright's skill. But the play's objective is, like Tommy's, sadly lacking.

Although we are eager to sympathize and admire a free spirit, an anarchic soul, an enemy to rules and regulations, a joyful and triumphant, life-loving and gifted personality, the fact remains that Tommy is empty when it comes to any intelligence in dealing with life as well as any passionate respect for anything other than self-interest. He says himself, "I want everything," and "I also think about blowing this country up so we can start all over again. I sort of dig this country, see?"(15) He is indeed a child, a flower child, one of his generation, who like so many speaking in the sixties found the an-swer in "blowing up the country." Tommy carries out his thought with his final act: he plants a bomb near a cop, wanders away to future pranks, and soon the bomb goes off. After the bomb explodes, the stage is empty, no cop anywhere to be seen.

One year after *Tommy Flowers* was produced at Yale, the twenty-seven-year-old flower child David Epstein wrote *Darkroom,* also pro-duced by the Yale Repertory Theater. The thesis of that play was that his generation could not develop because its rebellion was mindless. Liberty was misunderstood as license; sexual freedom was misunderstood as love; authority was misunderstood as tyranny.

Both Ruby and Tommy are monsters, quite different but oddly similar in their impact on those around them and in their self-obsession. In his introductory remarks to the play *And Things That Go Bump in the Night,* McNally says:

The Minneapolis experience was memorable on every level. Leueen MacGrath played Ruby with a malevolent intelligence, a passionate respect for evil, and a gallant bravery in the face of the inevitable that was light years beyond this poor attempt to describe it. Ruby is not a sympathetic part but Miss MacGrath was not afraid. That she moved the audience in her final moments is a matter of record. That she had the guts to wait till then, her very last speech, for the audience to "go" with her is an example of acting courage I have seem too seldom in our Freudian, Method . . . oriented theater. It was a noble, uncompromising performance. (6)

The audience, when it comes to Tommy Flowers, on the other hand, "goes" with him from the opening moment and never strays. The journey with Ruby is terrifying, rewarding, and unforgettable; the journey with Tommy Flowers is fleeting, delightful, and unsatisfying.

The arc from *And Things That Go Bump in the Night* to *Where Has Tommy Flowers Gone?* reflects the movement in the playwright— from an offensive, courageous, audacious spirit to one who opts for inoffensiveness, for appeal rather than impact on the unconscious and invisible. McNally presumably did not anticipate any actress's being willing to present Ruby as he had written her and thus his unreserved thrill and admiration for the performance by Leueen MacGrath. He had written a character from his deepest mystical, cannibalistic, barbaric yawp. On the other hand, he presumably never had a moment's doubt about James Coco endearing himself to the audience in *Next* nor about Robert Drivas captivating the audience with his performance as Tommy Flowers. McNally became more lovable than outrageous, more entertaining than inspiring. And so it goes.

Works Cited

Clurman, Harold. *The Collected Works*. New York: Applause Books, 1994.

Cohn, Ruby. *New American Dramatists: 1960–1980*. New York: Grove Press, 1982.

McNally, Terrence. *And Things That Go Bump in the Night*. New York: Dramatists Play
    Service, 1966.

———. *Fifteen Short Plays*. New Hampshire: Smith and Krause, 1994.

———. *Where Has Tommy Flowers Gone?* New York: Dramatists Play Service, 1972.

Chapter Three
Uneasy Transitions: Reassessing *The Lisbon Traviata* and Its Critics

Sam Abel

> The Lisbon Traviata *was never an easy play. It was hard to write, hard to cast, hard to rehearse, hard to perform, hard to get the critics to see what I was driving at.*
> — *Terrence McNally, Introduction to*
> Three Plays by Terrence McNally *(xii)*

None of Terrence McNally's plays has attracted more attention than *The Lisbon Traviata*, and none has elicited a more conflicted response from critics. The play has been enthusiastically admired and loudly reviled, often in the same breath. Critics praised its subtle plotting and condemned it as structurally flawed. They admired its vivid characterizations and criticized its characters' lack of motivation. They lauded its daring exploration of contemporary gay male issues and rejected its regressive stereotypes of gay men. Critics developed a love-hate relationship with *The Lisbon Traviata*, especially during its controversial 1989 New York production.

The firestorm of controversy over this production helped to propel McNally into the public spotlight; at the same time, the arguments make it difficult to come to any clear assessment of the play on its own merits. To make this process of evaluation even more complex, *The Lisbon Traviata* exists in multiple versions. McNally rewrote the play several times and devised two different conclusions, one murderous, the other murder-less. There are three published editions of the play, two of which McNally has, at various times, called the "definitive" version. McNally's "problem child" continues to make life difficult for anyone who wants to stage, read, or discuss the play.

In particular, four accusations leveled during the 1989 controversy have continued to haunt *The Lisbon Traviata*: that the play is not a single, unified work but rather two disjointed acts linked by the same characters; that neither ending for the play, not the violent one nor the bloodless one, works well but that the violent ending is especially problematic; that the play is regressive in its depiction of gay male life, relying on worn-out stereotypes of gay men as self-hating emotional cripples; and that the play is limited in its appeal to a small, gay and opera-loving coterie and is not accessible to a wider audience. These criticisms have, in the long run, done more to confuse discussions of the play than to enlighten them. Each is a loaded question, concealing a range of other, largely unresolvable, issues. In order to assess the long-term value of the play, the first task, then, is to sift through the critical debris left over from the 1989 controversy.

A Brief History of the Controversy

The original version of *The Lisbon Traviata* opened in June 1985 in New York in a showcase production at the Theatre Off Park. In the first act, two gay men, Stephen, a moderately successful playwright, and Mendy, his flamboyant friend, engage in bitchily comic repartee about sex and opera and especially about their favorite diva, Maria Callas. Their passion for opera covers the emptiness of their personal lives: Mendy is unhappily single, while Stephen's ten-year relationship with his lover, Mike, is on the rocks in part because Mike does not share his passion for opera. Mendy desperately wants to hear Stephen's pirated recording of *La Traviata*, performed by Callas in Lisbon in 1958; Stephen cannot get it because Mike has a new boyfriend, Paul, back at their apartment. Stranded, Stephen waits for a phone call from a potential date, which falls through.

The second act shifts to Mike and Stephen's apartment. Stephen returns home before Paul has left and proceeds to drive Paul away. After he leaves, Stephen and Mike get into a heated argument, at the climax of which Stephen stabs Mike rather than let him go off after Paul. As Mike dies, Stephen cradles him in his arms, while the voice of Callas is heard on the stereo. The showcase did not receive much critical attention nor an immediate commercial production. Mel Gussow gave it a noncommittal review in the *Times*; a more extensive and critical write-up by Julius Novick appeared in the *Village*

Voice, while John Simon offered a predictably negative assessment in *New York Magazine*. These reviews foreshadow the concerns that would be raised four years later about the play's structure and violent ending.

Supported by McNally's heightened public stock after the success of *Frankie and Johnny in the Clair de Lune* in 1987, the Manhattan Theatre Club opened a revised version of *The Lisbon Traviata* at City Center in the summer of 1989. McNally lengthened the play, reworked the dialogue, changed Stephen's profession from struggling playwright to established editor, made Mike a doctor, added references to the AIDS epidemic, and turned the final scene into a direct parallel of the last moments of *Carmen*. The overall shape of the play, however, remained intact, including the final act of violence. This production received much greater critical attention than the showcase, given the high-profile venue and McNally's recent commercial success. Gussow and Simon again reviewed the play, along with Mimi Kramer in the *New Yorker* and Michael Feingold in the *Village Voice*. Several background articles also appeared in the *Times*, including a feature about the play in the Sunday Arts and Leisure section and a profile of Nathan Lane, who played Mendy in the new production. Except for Feingold, the critics gave the play mixed reviews, praising many of its features but accusing it of being structurally disjointed and attacking its violent ending.

Despite these objections, the play moved from City Center to a more commercial run at the Promenade Theatre in October 1989. But under the pressure of the reviews (and presumably under pressure from his producers), McNally removed the act of violence from the last scene. In the new version, Stephen threatens to stab Mike, but he relents and lets Mike leave unharmed. The new ending did not, however, satisfy the critics. The *Times*, *Voice*, and *New York* all published reassessments, and new reviews appeared in *Time* and *The Nation*. These reviews perpetuated the controversy, again mixing admiration with attack, again aimed primarily at the last scene. The Promenade production ran for three months; the play was published, with the revised non-violent ending, in a volume along with *Frankie and Johnny* and *It's Only a Play*. In the introduction to this volume, McNally calls the non-violent version of the play "what I consider the definitive production" (*Three Plays*, xii).

A string of performances at regional theatres, mostly on the West Coast, followed the New York production. For these performances McNally once again revised the play. In this final revision, Mendy for the first time makes a brief appearance in the second act, and Mendy and Stephen have an even more intimate relationship than in earlier versions, including an acknowledgment by Stephen that the two should have been lovers. Most importantly, in the post-New York version, McNally reinstated the fatal stabbing of Mike, though he substantially shortened the scene. In an interview in the *San Francisco Examiner*, McNally again labels this version "definitive" (Rosenberg, 1); this version of the play was published and released for subsequent production by Dramatists Play Service.

The critical struggle over *The Lisbon Traviata* was more than a debate about the merits of the play; as I have argued elsewhere, the controversy laid bare a range of power struggles in the New York commercial theatre, particularly struggles over the representation of gay men on stage (Abel). *The Lisbon Traviata* clearly hit a nerve with the critics. The reviews are impassioned and at times self-contradictory, often raising more questions about the critics and their agendas than about the play. It is difficult, then, to take their accusations at face value. Each of the four major criticisms leveled against the play has a certain degree of validity, but each masks a range of deeper issues. What was really bothering the critics of *The Lisbon Traviata?*

One Play or Two?

The most persistent criticism of *The Lisbon Traviata* is that the two acts of the play do not form a unified whole, that McNally has written, in effect, two different plays united by common characters. Stephen and Mendy's witty repartee about sex and opera is, in this view, a campy comedy, albeit a bitter one; Stephen and Mike's bloody argument is a domestic tragedy with operatic overtones. This complaint first appeared in the reviews of the 1985 showcase and persisted throughout the 1989 controversy and in subsequent discussions of the play. For example, Gussow in 1985 states that the play "begins as a comedy . . . it ends as an impassioned dramatic equivalent of grand opera" ("Tale"); he repeats this assessment in his first 1989 review: "McNally has written the theatrical equivalent of an operatic double bill—an opéra bouffe followed by a tragic denoue-

ment" ("Agony"). John Simon is somewhat more blunt in condemn-
ing this tragic/comic split: "*The Lisbon Traviata* . . . has a ravishingly
comic first act and an unconvincingly glued-on, melodramatic second" ("Anti-Romances"). John Clum, writing about the play after
the controversy, repeats this formula in his generally negative assessment: "The first act, set in Mendy's ornate, campy world, is comedy. . . . The second act . . . veers toward operatic pathos" (261–2).
McNally himself has reinforced this perception of the play's split
structure; he describes *The Lisbon Traviata* as "an opera buffa that
ends up verismo tragedy" (*Three Plays*, xiii).

In retrospect, this criticism of duality makes little sense. *The
Lisbon Traviata* is not two different plays glued randomly together;
the events of the second act clearly grow out of the situations established in the first. The two-play argument is valid only on the most
superficial level: the second act takes place in a different location;
characters only mentioned in the first act appear in the second; and
the tone of the second act contrasts sharply to that of the first. But
McNally is careful, especially in the revised versions, to prepare this
shift in tone; the first act provides clear suggestions of Stephen's underlying bitterness. Nothing happens in Act II that is not grounded
firmly in Act I. And *The Lisbon Traviata* is hardly the only example
in contemporary dramatic literature of a play that shifts mood sharply
from the comic to the serious; David Rabe's *Streamers*, John Guare's
The House of Blue Leaves, and other contemporary classics have employed this technique to great critical acclaim. If anything, the uncomfortable mixing of tragic and comic elements is the norm for
post-Beckettian drama, a reflection of the violent undercurrents in
late twentieth-century society.

If the play's structure does not support the claim of duality, why
have critics leveled this accusation? My sense is that critics used this
argument to mask a less acceptable complaint, a wish that the play
had taken a different course than the one McNally chose. The first
act of the play is highly amusing, filled with biting repartee and
brilliant one-liners; in the second act the humor falls out of the
bitchiness, and the play becomes painful to watch. It is not that the
first act does not prepare the way for the second; it does. But the
critics resisted following the play to its logical conclusion; they wanted
a second act that offered more of the pleasures of the first. Charles

Marowitz, reviewing the Los Angeles production, expresses this disappointment with the wrenching second act: "The pain and plausibility of that situation, earnest as it is, simply cannot compete with the supernal comedy of the previous scene. Although there is no structural reason why a play cannot go from comedy to pathos, there has to be an equivalence of quality between both parts to avoid a letdown. The shoals of McNally's graver situation are too many degrees below the peaks of his former levity." Marowitz implies that McNally's theatrical skills fall short in the second act; I would argue that the melodramatic intensity of the final act does, in fact, parallel the comic intensity of the first and that the letdown comes not from the play's failures but from the critics' desire not to accept the inevitable pain of the play's ending.

In fact, it is clear from many of the critics that they wanted a play about Mendy, not Stephen. Mendy is an appealing and sympathetic character; as Steven Drukman has argued, he elicits complex processes of audience identification, and he embodies the play's eponymous search for the elusive Lisbon *Traviata* recording (26). Many reviews focus on Mendy's appeal, especially in Nathan Lane's performance. The *Times* ran a long article about Lane but had no equivalent coverage of Anthony Heald, who played Stephen. But Mendy disappears from the play in the second act, and we are left alone with Stephen. Stephen is a difficult person, and by the end of the play it is very hard to like him, no matter in which version of the ending. If Mendy has personal problems, he at least makes them entertaining. Stephen's overwhelming anger and bitterness are far less attractive, and he lacks Mendy's survival skills. By leaving us with Stephen, McNally forces us into a much uglier world.

Mimi Kramer expresses this desire to see a different story than the one McNally chooses to tell: "Mendy never reappears, and that is strange; everything about the structure of the play suggests he will. . . . It's easy to imagine a 'Lisbon Traviata' that ends with Mendy's discovery that the sought-after recording doesn't exist. Mendy and Stephen are as much foils for each other as equal partners in the drama: we want a final confrontation between them; we want to recognize that the two obscure objects of his desire are equally mythical" (76). Actually, there is very little in the first act to suggest that Mendy will play a significant role later on; as amusing as he is, he is a static figure, with no relationships that could develop into any kind of denouement, tragic or comic. Kramer's attempt to rewrite the play is utter nonsense and has nothing to do with McNally's dramatic vision (and, arguably, is thinly veiled homophobia, implying that all love between gay men is necessarily "mythical"). Kramer is not criticizing McNally's play; she is criticizing a play McNally had no intention of writing.

In the final revised version McNally did, in fact, bring Mendy briefly into the second act, apparently in an attempt to appease the critics. But this scene is unnecessary and disruptive; Mendy has no place in the world of the second act. Mendy is isolated; his only access to the outside world is the telephone. Mike and Paul live in the streets of New York; they go out to a movie and for pizza, drive to Harlem, and take the subway. Though we do not see their movements, through narration we follow their free movement in the city throughout the play. McNally's point is that Stephen, by moving into Mendy's isolated world of opera, has lost his ability to function in the real world of Mike and Paul. When Stephen leaves Mendy's apartment he loses his bearings, and this imbalance results in his final act of violence. The vivid image of Mendy lingers over the second act, but his physical presence undermines the play's structure.

Ultimately, the real problem with the comic/tragic dichotomy argument is that the first act of *The Lisbon Traviata* is not a comedy at all; it is an exploration of two empty lives, one of them on the brink of dissolution, and of the terrors of finding love in the era of AIDS. It has a lot of funny lines but none of the underlying structural elements of comedy. As Thomas Disch points out in his review in *The Nation*, the tragedy of the second act is implicit in the humor of the first act; David Román argues that "the tragedy embedded in *The Lisbon Traviata* . . . emerges from the universe of the first comic half of the play" (307). Even Gussow, who is among the most vocal critics of the play's "split" structure, answers his own complaint by admitting that "the first act is tragedy in the guise of comedy" ("Agony"). *The Lisbon Traviata* is not a tragedy appended to a comedy. Stephen's story, the serious depiction of a life in disarray, is there from the first moments of the play. It is a tribute to McNally's skill as a dramatist that he can draw us into this painful story through the first act's comic banter, so that we will stick around to watch the intensely uncomfortable events of the second act.

To Kill or Not to Kill?

If the most frequent critiques of *The Lisbon Traviata* concerned its structure, the most vehement debates arose about its violent ending. Stephen's murder of Mike dominated the reviews of the June 1989 production, and the mainstream critics were consistent in their condemnation of the final scene. Most argued that McNally was trying to give the play an operatic ending, and that this conclusion did not fit the play's realistic setting and characters. Gussow observes: "While the violent conclusion may seem inevitable in the context of opera, it is not convincing in this domestic drama" ("Agony"). Kramer admires the play's structure until the last ten minutes: "Then everything goes haywire: Stephen pulls a knife on his lover, and—death before desertion—the play ends on a note of tragedy and betrayal. . . . The trouble is that the material of 'The Lisbon Traviata' is not the stuff of which grand opera is made" (76). Novick in 1985 similarly finds the ending stylistically incongruous; he says that McNally has written "a realistic play about a modern homosexual American man who loves with the same intensity as the operatic heroines, the Normas and the Medeas, that Maria Callas played. . . . Perhaps what Mr. McNally is attempting is not possible. . . . A realistic play cannot contain Stephen's passionate fury" (96).

These complaints are valid to the degree that McNally intends the murder to be operatic in scope and effect. The final scene is clearly a case of life imitating opera; this effect is particularly clear in the 1989 version, in which Mendy and Stephen frequently play-act operatic death scenes and where the ending mimics the final scene of *Carmen* virtually word for word. Will Crutchfield, in a New York *Times* pre-production profile of McNally, observes that the playwright's object was to "pursue our grand obsessions to their 19th-century climaxes." But does such an operatic ending belong in the living rooms of upscale Manhattan apartment buildings? Is *The Lisbon Traviata*, as the critics imply, a traditional example of domestic realism, and if so, is murder appropriate to this sort of play?

In response to the argument that the murder is unrealistic, McNally argues: "It is clearly not a well-made play in which the first act prepares us for everything that happens in the second. Yesterday did not prepare me for what happened today. Life is a lousy playwright that way. I was merely trying to reflect that in *The Lisbon Traviata*" (*Three Plays*, xii). This explanation is, however, problematic, because theatre, even realistic theatre, demands more structure than real life. More importantly, the first act does prepare for the second. The critics' complaint is not that the murder is unprepared (several of the reviews note that McNally clearly foreshadows the event) but that it is an extreme act, one that seems inappropriate within the limits of realistic decorum.

I would argue that by labeling *The Lisbon Traviata* as "domestic realism," the critics were again trying to rewrite the play, to view it as the stylistic equivalent to McNally's previous success, *Frankie and Johnny in the Clair de Lune*. This earlier work is undeniably an example of domestic realism in the film and television mode, an intimate study of two average people wrestling with familiar, everyday issues about sexual relationships. *Frankie and Johnny* is a comfortable play, not in any way threatening to standard dramatic norms (and therefore McNally's only script to get an immediate Hollywood production). But *The Lisbon Traviata* is a very different play from *Frankie and Johnny*. It is not comfortable, and it is not about average people in recognizable situations. Mike and Paul are pretty normal, but Mendy and Stephen are extreme, and they behave in extreme ways. *The Lisbon Traviata* is only realistic to the degree that *verismo* operas like *Tosca* and *I Pagliacci* are realistic; it employs the external trappings of realism in setting, character, and situation, but it depicts situations bordering on the edges of human behavior. The play is not a case of domestic realism turned to opera. It is operatic in scope, in its comedy and in its violence, from the beginning. *The Lisbon Traviata* is not realism; it is tragedy overlaid with farce, and neither tragedy nor farce are realistic genres.

The necessity of the final act of violence was powerfully illustrated by the critical response when McNally removed the murder. A few critics praised the new ending, but most found it a substantial disappointment. Gussow comments that the new ending does not solve the play's problems; Henry in *Time* argues that the non-violent ending feels "anticlimactic, void of release." Simon comments: "Now all that is left is a dismal parting, a Brechtian silent scream, and the not exactly new notion that life goes on. This is saying less" ("Some-thing"). Without the final murder, the operatic-scale tensions built up throughout the play have no resolution.

McNally, then, called the critics' bluff by removing the murder; in doing so, he revealed that their objection arose not from a struc-tural flaw in the play but again out of a desire to rewrite the play. This kind of debate about how a play should end is an unusual subject in theatre criticism; it is not normally the prerogative of the critic to make such suggestions. The only major parallel example is the debate surrounding the ending of Tennessee Williams' *Cat on a Hot Tin Roof*, another play with a heavy gay thematic. In both cases, "mainstream" authorities rejected the playwright's bleaker view in favor of a more upbeat and less daring ending. After he had restored the original ending, McNally observed in an interview that the non-violent ending was too sentimental, too easy for the audience. "If this were the Elizabethan or the Jacobean period, no one would ques-tion the ending. I think it's the passion in this play that frightens and startles people" (Rosenberg). The mainstream critics found the gay subject matter sufficiently uncomfortable by itself and so re-jected the even greater discomfort of Mike's murder.

This murder is fraught with implications, which further com-plicate the question of the play's ending. On the most basic level, if Stephen is the protagonist, the character with whom we are sup-posed to identify, then the murder presents a frightening reflection of the audience. If a person like Stephen is capable of murder, does that mean we all contain the potential for violence? Do self-destruc-tive impulses turn so easily onto the people we love? Is modern soci-ety so close to the brink? Arguably, McNally's answer to all of these questions is "yes," and that answer asks a great deal of any audience. The murder does not get any easier if Stephen is viewed not as a reflection of the general audience but of the gay community. In this reading, the violent ending is troubling because Mike represents a more healthy, positive vision of gay life. If Stephen kills Mike, it implies that the gay community is self-destructive and that the psy-chological baggage of the past continues to haunt the present.

Even more troubling, McNally does not permit any sense of redemption from this death; Mike's death provides an emotional release for the play's operatic tensions, but it does not offer the kind of transcendent closure found in opera's tragic death scenes. As Román and Drukman both argue, *The Lisbon Traviata* is in many ways a play about AIDS, and Mike's death evokes the persistent presence of death hovering over the New York gay community. Román states: "given the fact that in this finale, Stephen's lover—a doctor and the only character in the play with any AIDS awareness—now lies dying suggests that gay male identities are further threatened within the world of the play" (311). This picture can be especially troubling for a sympathetic straight audience; as Drukman argues, a gay-identified audience can use its experience to fashion a more complex and nuanced reading of McNally's vision of death within the gay community. Without such a context or a sense of redemption at the end, the murder may appear to a straight audience as a "real" depiction of gay self-destructiveness. If the murder of Mike is an appropriate, even necessary, ending to *The Lisbon Traviata*, it is not an easy ending for any audience member to watch.

Insight or Stereotype?

The question of gay and straight readings of the final scene raises another critical complaint about *The Lisbon Traviata*, the accusation that the play reproduces limiting, worn-out stereotypes of gay men. This complaint was less central to the 1989 controversy but has surfaced regularly in subsequent considerations of the play. In particular, several critics have argued that Stephen and Mendy reproduce the stereotype of the self-hating homosexual canonized in *The Boys in the Band*. They use opera, these critics argue, as a psychological crutch, a way to fill the void created by their failed love lives. Clum, for example, observes that "Mendy and Stephen . . . are holdovers from an earlier time, self-hating gay men who use elements of gay culture to encase themselves in a bearable world" (259). These characters, Clum argues, have no significant connection to the problems of gay life in New York such as AIDS and violence; they are so wrapped up in their own psychological problems that they "are oblivious to real suffering" (261).

David Román voices an even more forceful indictment of the play's vision of gay male life: "In *The Lisbon Traviata*, McNally stages characters locked in the gridlock of masterplots and their resulting archetypal pathologies. McNally's own struggle to write a play that demonstrates what might be called the operas of everyday life fails to let his characters, gay men in the midst of an epidemic, recognize that opera is opera and everyday life something much more negotiable than either Mendy or Stephen can fathom. . . . McNally seems to see no place for subversion within the possibilities of gay identity" (310–11). An equally negative, if less analytical, attack comes from Laurie Stone in her *Village Voice* review of the November 1989 production. Stone entirely dismisses McNally's vision of troubled gay relationships: "We're given only a clichéd sketch of the relationship Stephen is losing; it's not even clear what opera means to him. More problematic, Michael ousts Stephen from their shared apartment in order to have sex with his new lover, but Michael is never charged with cruelty, or even boorishness. The play views this shabby treatment as sophisticated—and as a given in gay relationships."

On the other hand, Disch, the only reviewer of the 1989 production who self-identifies as gay, sees himself in the play, not stereotypes: "I felt as some blacks must have at *A Raisin in the Sun*, not just the basic pleasure all good theatre yields but the special glow of hearing one's own particular, quotidian truths expressed with force and dignity and consummate artistry" (766). Drukman, in "Gay-Gazing at *The Lisbon Traviata*," does not go so far in his praise for the play's depiction of gay life, but he does feel that the play has value for the gay male spectator. He argues that the play does not so much depict negative stereotypes as that it offers "a cautionary tale of gay men's desires to escape reality in the unfathomable age of AIDS" (31). Critics, then, have sharply split in their assessment of the play's depiction of gay male characters and the proximity of these characters to the actual lives of urban gay men.

In his *Times* interview with Crutchfield, McNally seems defensive about the possibility of Stephen and Mendy being viewed as negative stereotypes of gay opera fans. He denounces the term "opera queen" and asserts: "It's a play about four gay men, not a statement about gays or gay culture. It could be about four heterosexuals obsessed with baseball statistics." (Nathan Lane, in his *Times* interview with Glenn Collins, makes virtually the same statement, including the reference to baseball.) In practical terms, of course, *The Lisbon Traviata* could not be about four heterosexual men obsessed with baseball, because heterosexual men would not be affected by the sexual tensions that drive McNally's play. McNally uses baseball here as a marker of butchness, a tactic to deflect the issue of gay stereotypes. In denying that the play incorporates these stereotypes, McNally, it seems, wants to sidestep the troubling question raised by Román and other critics, that Stephen and Mendy embody a pre-liberation view of gay life.

There is no question that *The Lisbon Traviata* evokes familiar stereotypes of gay men. The most obvious example, despite McNally's objection, is the stereotype of the flamboyant opera queen. As much as McNally wants to deny the term, the stereotype is, as Wayne Koestenbaum's book *The Queen's Throat* illustrates, alive and well in the gay community, and Stephen and Mendy are dead-on portraits of the character. If the excesses of *The Lisbon Traviata* take the play out of the realm of realism, then this atmosphere of excess carries the play's central characters into the realm of stereotypes. Further, McNally firmly ties his vision of the opera queen to the image of the self-hating gay man. In his descriptions of the characters, McNally says of Paul that he "likes himself," implying that the other characters do not. McNally's opera queens clearly are not happy people, particularly about their sex lives.

But while Mendy and Stephen bear close resemblance to Michael and Donald in *The Boys in the Band*, McNally's characters differ from the earlier stereotype in two important ways. First, Mendy and Stephen may be self-hating gay men, but they, unlike Michael and Donald, do not hate themselves specifically *because* they are gay. McNally does not imply that all gay men are self-hating, in the way that *The Boys in the Band* does; there is no equivalent speech to Michael's climactic "If we could just learn not to hate ourselves quite so very much" (178). If Mendy and Stephen hate themselves, it is due to the combined pressures of AIDS and life in New York, not the simple fact of being gay. And even if Mendy and Stephen seem inextricably linked to the older stereotype, McNally creates a sharp generational split in the play; the younger the character, the less tied he is to self-hatred. Mendy and Stephen, the older characters, cannot escape from their psychological baggage, and Mike, slightly younger, gets destroyed in the process, but Paul, the youngest one, gets out. If the present is bleak, Paul represents hope for the future.

The second difference is that while McNally evokes the stereotype of the self-hating gay man, he makes several significant reversals in the picture. Both Mendy and Stephen embody the opera queen stereotype, but only Mendy (who is less self-hating than Stephen) is truly flamboyant. Stephen, who knows more about opera, does not fit the behavioral description of the stereotype; as Mendy points out, Stephen is too butch to know so much about opera. More importantly, in the standard stereotype, if Stephen is the self-hating gay man, then he should be the victim of violence, not its perpetrator. By having Stephen commit murder, McNally turns the *Boys in the Band* stereotype on its head, making the scene all the more troubling for audiences looking for a comfortable vision of gay existence.

The Lisbon Traviata appeared at a transitional moment in the depiction of gay men in the American theatre. Prior to the 90s, there were few plays about gay men in mainstream theatre, and those that made it to Broadway relied on heavily stereotyped portrayals of gay men as self-hating cripples, AIDS victims, or drag queens. Many gay viewers wanted *The Lisbon Traviata*, as one of the few plays by an established mainstream playwright to depict an exclusively gay world, to show a positive view of gay life. Instead it offers a difficult and painful picture, centered around the problematic character of Stephen. There is an inevitable tendency for audiences, gay or straight, to view gay characters as representative of all gay people, especially in the absence of other more positive representations; this tendency plagues all representations of minority populations in popular culture. The condemnation of the gay characters in *The Lisbon Traviata* arose largely out of frustration with this situation.

As McNally makes clear in his baseball statement, he does not intend Mendy and Stephen to represent all gay men. Nor is McNally, fundamentally, a playwright with a political agenda; unlike Tony Kushner or even Harvey Fierstein, he is not out to change the minds of his audience or to get them to live their lives differently. But the tendency to read the play as representative of gay life is both inevitable and understandable. The same situation was true of *The Boys in the Band* in its original production; Crowley's play has recently enjoyed a revival in popularity, now that there is enough historical distance to see the play not as representative of the present moment but of a past situation. The further we travel from the situation in 1989, and the more positive images of gay men that appear on Broadway, the easier it will be to view *The Lisbon Traviata* and its characters the way McNally intended.

A Play for Everyone?

The problem of gay representation in *The Lisbon Traviata* raises a final critical question, whether the play has a broad popular appeal or whether instead it is accessible only to the kinds of people depicted in the play, specifically gay men with a knowledge of opera. This question actually breaks down into two separate complaints. The first, and more easily addressed, is that the barrage of opera references in the first act makes the play so obscure that only people who know opera will understand it; Stephen's line "I'm not butch; Risë Stevens is butch" is only funny if you know who Risë Stevens is. Clum, for example, argues: "On one level, *The Lisbon Traviata* is a satire on opera queens filled with diva jokes that only opera queens would understand" (262). In reviewing the 1985 showcase, Gussow remarks that the play's atmosphere is "both esoteric and hermetic," implying that non-opera-going fans would have trouble getting access to the world of the first act. Other critics raise the issue more ambivalently; Kramer finds that "'The Lisbon Traviata' . . . is only partly a play for and about opera buffs. . . . It has a governing conceit that raises it above the level of coterie entertainment" (75).

There is no question that the play depends, especially in the first act, on the arcane language of opera. But I would argue that, despite Clum's warnings, the opera references are not a major deterrent to understanding the play. McNally does a good job of providing the audience with enough information to figure out what is going on, especially in the later versions. And if some audience members feel alienated by these references, McNally offers Mike and Paul to ground their feelings of distance. On the other hand, the opera references do have the effect of sharply shifting the way an audience member might respond to the play. If you can follow Mendy and Stephen's repartee, you are more likely to identify with them, and therefore to see Stephen as more sympathetic; if you can't follow him, he becomes a much more annoying character. Lack of access to the opera references thus could substantially affect the more central issues outlined previously, the appropriateness of the murder and the perception of gay stereotypes.

Considerably more sensitive is the accusation that *The Lisbon Traviata*, by exclusively depicting a world of gay men, is not accessible to a straight audience. The plays that brought McNally to wide public acclaim and that immediately preceded *The Lisbon Traviata*, *It's Only a Play* and *Frankie and Johnny in the Clair de Lune*, deal primarily with straight characters; *The Lisbon Traviata* depicts only gay male characters, an issue noted by some critics. Some of the reviewers clearly felt put off; Gussow's remark that the play is "esoteric and hermetic" can equally refer to its gay content. Gussow in the same review comments that the play's sexual "frankness may offend some theatregoers." Simon notes that "Homosexual sex is graphically evoked, shocking at least two of my colleagues audibly" ("All Wet"). The play was first published in an anthology of "gay and lesbian plays," and Clum includes it in his book about gay male drama, reinforcing the perception of the work as a "gay play." On the other hand, Feingold, reviewing the play for the *Village Voice*, with its heavy gay readership, remarks, "McNally has deepened the debate so it could apply to *any* pairing: That the pair happens to be two men simply helps us to read the questions it raises more clearly because differences of gender don't come into it."

These comments raise the thorny issue of whether there is such a thing as a "gay play," and if there is, how such a play relates to "gay" and "straight" audiences (if those terms have any meaning). In his article on *The Lisbon Traviata*, Drukman argues that, due to its subject matter and structure, McNally's play is, in fact, more accessible to a gay viewer than to a straight one. He suggests that the critics had problems with the play, especially with the shift from comedy to tragedy, because they viewed the play from a heterosexual perspective. It is easier, Drukman argues, for a spectator employing a "gay gaze" to negotiate the shift in tone between the two acts (29–32). On the other hand, the play certainly found support from a mainstream (i.e., "straight") audience, who found enough of interest in the play to support a major commercial production. And McNally's subsequent success on Broadway with *Love! Valour! Compassion!*, which deals just as exclusively with gay issues, illustrates the limitations of the "gay play" argument.

The problem, then, is not really whether *The Lisbon Traviata* is or is not accessible to a straight-identified audience; it clearly is, though not necessarily in the same way that it is to a gay-identified audience. The problem comes with the way mainstream critics employed the concept of a "gay play" during the 1989 run. The suggestion that a straight audience cannot accept a vision of gay life as "universal" is nothing but veiled homophobia, an example of the standard ploy used to delegitimate the success of a work that does not conform to mainstream sensibilities. One of the great achievements of *The Lisbon Traviata* is that it was able to demonstrate that a "gay play" could in fact attract a wider audience. As with the question of representing gay characters, *The Lisbon Traviata's* appearance at a transitional moment in the relationship between gay and straight culture clouded the debate on this issue. The language and images of gay life have become increasingly a part of mainstream culture since 1989; the more this process goes forward, the less valid this complaint becomes.

The Lisbon Traviata is a play in the middle: in the middle of changes in the public representation of gay men, in the middle of McNally's shift from Off-Broadway to mainstream playwright, in the middle of familiar theatrical genres. The attacks leveled against the play during its New York productions arose less from the play's merits or flaws than from the tensions between the play and its historical circumstances. As McNally observes, it is a difficult play, because it raises a wide range of uncomfortable, sometimes painful, issues without opting for easy answers and because it came to the stage at a difficult time. *The Lisbon Traviata* is certainly not without its flaws. But it is a daring work, one that laid bare the raw nerves of American culture in the late 80s. It captures a significant historical moment of transition, both in McNally's career and in the American commercial theatre; therefore, it deserves further production and critical exploration that transcends the largely fruitless and circular debates that plagued its original production.

Works Cited

Abel, Sam. "The Death of Queens: *The Lisbon Traviata* Controversy and Gay Male Representation in the Mainstream Theatre," *Theatre History Studies* 16 (1996).

Clum, John. *Acting Gay: Male Homosexuality in Modern Drama*. New York: Columbia University Press, 1992.

Collins, Glenn. "A Comic Triumph as a Tragic Callas Worshipper." *New York Times*, 14 June 1989: C19.

Crowley, Mart. *The Boys in the Band*. New York: Farrar, Straus & Giroux, 1968.

Crutchfield, Will. "Dishing About Divas and Other Opera Chat." *New York Times*, 4
     June 1989: II, 5+.
Disch, Thomas M. "The Lisbon Traviata." *The Nation*, 18 December 1989: 766–7.
Drukman, Steven. "Gay-Gazing at *The Lisbon Traviata*, or: How Are Things in *Tosca,
     Norma?*" *Theatre Topics* 5.1 (1995): 23–34.
Feingold, Michael. "Camp Followers." *Village Voice*, 13 June 1989: 97.
Gussow, Mel. "Agony and Ecstasy of an Opera Addiction." *New York Times*, 7 June
     1989: 21.
———. "A New, Non-Violent Ending for 'Lisbon Traviata'." *New York Times*, 1 Novem-
     ber 1989: 22.
———. "Stage: 'Lisbon Traviata,' Tale of Two Opera Fans." *New York Times*, 19 June
     1985: III, 14.
Henry, William A., III. "Downbeat Duo." *Time*, 13 November 1989: 120.
Klein, Alvin. "McNally's Plays Take Diverse Paths." *New York Times*, 19 November
     1989: sec. 21, 25.
Koestenbaum, Wayne. *The Queen's Throat: Opera, Homosexuality, and the Mystery of
     Desire*. New York: Poseidon Press, 1993.
Kramer, Mimi. "The Manhattan Traviata." *New Yorker*, 19 June 1989: 74–6.
Marowitz, Charles. "Los Angeles in Review: The Lisbon Traviata." *Theatre Week*, 31
     December 1990: 38–39.
McNally, Terrence. *The Lisbon Traviata*. New York: Dramatists Play Service, 1992.
———. *Three Plays by Terrence McNally*. New York: Plume, 1990.
Novick, Julius. "Ave Maria." *Village Voice*, 2 July 1985: 95–6.
Román, David. "'It's My Party and I'll Die If I Want To!': Gay Men, AIDS, and the Circu-
     lation of Camp in U.S. Theatre." *Theatre Journal* 44.3 (1992): 305–328.
Rosenberg, Scott. "Playwright Dreams of the Road." *San Francisco Examiner*, 21
     October 1990: E-1.
Shewey, Don. *Out Front*. New York: Grove Press, 1988.
Simon, John. "All Wet." *New York Magazine*, 15 July 1985: 67–9.
———. "Anti-Romances." *New York Magazine*, 19 June 1989: 71–3.
———. "Something Borrowed, Something Blah." *New York Magazine*, 13 November
     1989: 130–1.
Stone, Laurie. "Cameos," *Village Voice*, 7 November 1989: 111.

Chapter Four
Lips Together, Teeth Apart:
Bodies in Search of a
Dramatic Form

Stephen Watt

> *"The body"... has become the latest shibboleth of literary theory,*
> *particularly west of the Rockies, where essays on the body are*
> *churned out of PC's with the same demonic rigor that the bodies*
> *of their authors are submitted to the tortures of the gym.*
> —*Maud Ellmann,* The Hunger Artists

> *I have a picture of a starving child in Somalia over my desk....*
> *The child has fallen forward on his haunches, he's so weak from*
> *hunger, he can barely lift his head.*
> —*Buzz,* Love! Valour! Compassion!

As the cast members of Terrence McNally's *Lips Together, Teeth Apart*
were settling into their parts—its inaugural production opened in
May of 1991—newsstands were being stocked with magazines that
brought the AIDS crisis front and center into the national consciousness. This spring and summer, though, the discourse on AIDS was
different, in part because the body in pain was different and because
the context in which this body was situated was vastly more terrifying. In its July 1, 1991, issue, for example, *Newsweek* strategically
positioned a photograph of a then-sixty-five-pound Kimberly Bergalis
in her deathbed over the bold-faced title, "Doctors and AIDS." A
medium close-up of her wasted frame and tense face was spread over
a page and a half, dominating the text that attempted to explain
both. In the lower right-hand corner of the photograph, a terse epigraph seemed to say it all: "I'm dying guys. Goodbye." Predictably
enough, the accompanying narrative began with a chronicle of a
body in horrible decline: "At 65 pounds, she is half her normal body
weight. Her skin is chalk white and her eyes stare blankly at the

television. . . . In late March the 23-year-old Bergalis took long walks on the beach; now she can barely lift her arms" (49). We all know the story. We all know that she was infected by her dentist, as were several other patients interviewed in a made-for-media nightmare covered by nearly every major magazine, every television network. And, in an age where surveys drive public policy and political agendas alike, we also know that because of cases like hers over 90% of Americans in the summer of 1991 believed doctors should be required to disclose serious medical conditions to patients—and that patients should likewise be compelled to inform health-care workers of such diagnoses as HIV (although how one can be required to reveal such information and still retain the right to privacy is another matter).

Some eighteen months later, another image of the body in pain commanded our attention. Like Kimberly Bergalis too ill to lift her arms, the Somali child Buzz recalls in *Love! Valour! Compassion!* (1994) is too weak to raise his head. Much as her ravaged body became *the* site for discourse on AIDS and the crisis in health care in the summer of 1991, the child's wasted frame communicated the horror of famine to millions of us. So, if Maud Ellmann is right, if the body *has* become the "shibboleth" of both cultural theory and literary study (3), it also serves as more than a password into the rarefied atmospheres of postmodernity, performativity, and gender "troubles" (although these are quite salutary intellectual airs to take in from time to time). The body afflicted by AIDS, famine, and the cultural neuroses that lead to anorexia nervosa is a material, quotidian reality in a global culture some describe as postmodern. Further, as Ellmann and Susan Jeffords delineate in their very different ways, the body can also be wielded as a political weapon, from the emaciated forms of hunger strikers in Northern Ireland's Armagh prison for women to the muscular, Schwarzeneggerian bodies that Jeffords argues subtended the cultural mythology of the Reagan White House. In this mythology, the Reagan administration projected images of the "hard body . . . for a rearticulation of masculine strength and power through internal, personal, and family-oriented values" (13). We also know this story, mainly through analogies and sound bites: Reagan (and Oliver North) playing Rambo ready to take on the evil Empire anywhere in the world; George Bush playing Dirty Harry when telling voters, "Read my lips." Theoretical *and* popular discourses in the 1980s and 90s, it would seem, have not made just *any* body a "shibboleth" or academic fetish; rather, they have mapped the boundaries of representations that are so much a part of our everyday life they are in danger of being taken for granted. However striking or manipulable for repressive or propagandistic purposes, photographs of Kimberly Bergalis and Somali children thus constitute only two instances of an ongoing cultural obsession with bodies and the historical contingencies of their representation.

Terrence McNally and many, perhaps most, of his characters share this obsession with both the beauty and fragility of the human body—and, finally, with its inevitable diminution. And, although the body with AIDS is a major concern of such plays as *Love! Valour! Compassion!*, it hardly amounts to McNally's only commentary on the topic. For whether it is Johnny in *Frankie and Johnny in the Clair de Lune* (1987) cataloguing the "supremely great sights of life"— which include "a woman combing and fixing her hair" (17), Frankie's "wonderful breasts" (5) and "beautiful pussy" (23)—or Stephen in *The Lisbon Traviata* (1989) desperately offering intimate Polaroids of him and Mike to Paul, Mike's new lover, the body seems the principal text in, or at times the complex subtext of, McNally's plays, as knotted and rife for textualization as Gregory's aging dancer's legs in *Love! Valour! Compassion!*. "I never really looked at your body before," Perry tells Gregory. "It's amazing" (77). So is Ramon's physique in *Love! Valour! Compassion!* and that of an attractive gay man Chloe spies in *Lips Together, Teeth Apart*: "There, on the beach, in the thong bikini. Joan Rivers was right about those things. It does look like he's flossing his ass" (45). In the same scene the gay body, toned and potent, is juxtaposed to a husbandly physique in which such attributes are on the wane. Chloe wonders, "[D]on't straight men think we have eyes? Don't they occasionally look at themselves in the mirror. . . . (To John) Give me twenty push-ups. Let's go. The party's over" (45). But in more serious moments in *Lips Together, Teeth Apart* we learn of the male body suffering from more than middle-aged spread—John's incipient esophageal cancer, for instance. Less fatal but nonetheless formidable are Sam's maladies, of which he reminds his sister Chloe earlier: the anxiety of two mortgages, an impending hernia operation (a procedure Johnny in *Frankie and*

Johnny has undergone), and the fears of both impotence and abandonment. "Sometimes I have to think about someone else when I'm with [Sally] because I'm afraid I won't stay hard if I don't" (43), Sam admits in an interior monologue, yet he is "most afraid" of losing her and devastated by her betrayal with John. Bodies and desires, the search for gratification and escape from fear, love and death—all exist in time, even at its end, and it is the playwright's occupation to find a dramatic form with which to represent all of these.

Lips Together, Teeth Apart, a title suggestive of a certain fascination with the body in all of its conditions and with all of its complexities, is the result of McNally's attempts to craft, from a variety of prior conventions and generic shapes, an appropriate form for both "hard bodies" and those in decline. Stated more simply, what kind of dramatic form can both register the pain of AIDS *and* portray the beauty of the body and desire that exist side by side with such a catastrophe? (I use "catastrophe" here not merely in the common sense of a tragic or calamitous event, but also in the sense developed by theorists of the catastrophic to designate processes of sudden, unpredictable change: a discontinuity, irregularity, or rupture in a homeostatic system.)[1] This dimension of McNally's project—the formal ways he attempts to commingle comic celebration with an almost nihilistic sense of the catastrophic—is the subject of much of what follows, particularly insofar as it relates to that most elusive cultural and theoretical construct, postmodernism, which at times rears its problematic head in critical responses to McNally's work.

What I hope to show is that McNally's insistence on the materiality of the body poses a problem for reading his work as postmodern, especially that sense of postmodernity or a "society of the spectacle" adumbrated by Jean Baudrillard and Guy DeBord. For while the body can be simulated and perfected in the hollow emptiness of the image, thus rendered hyperreal, and while McNally's characters often want to escape from the real into a world of music, opera, or pastoral beauty, bodies in McNally are seldom transformed into "simple images" which then become "real beings" (DeBord, 18).[2] Perhaps this is true because the spectacle is, in both Baudrillard's and DeBord's critiques, the product of an "economic system founded on isolation," on a technology (television in particular) that selects goods as "weapons for a constant reinforcement of the conditions of isolation of 'lonely crowds'" (DeBord, 28), and McNally's characters, for the most part, seek connection with a larger community and evince little interest in mass culture. Dance, opera, theatre—all of these performances privilege the body incarnate, not its filmic or televised image, and these are the cultural forms to which many of McNally's characters are deeply committed (even if, in Chloe's case, this commitment is to rather banal musical theatre). It is within this theoretical and thematic framework that bodies meet dramatic form in my reading of *Lips Together, Teeth Apart*, a reading that also suggests in the most provisional way the substantial difficulties (pun intended) which AIDS and the material body pose for theorizations of postmodernity relying upon such concepts as simulation, the abolition of difference, and hyper-reality in contemporary culture.

Formal Hybridity

Depending upon what thesis or reviewerly opinion one credits, *Lips Together, Teeth Apart* possesses a kind of hybrid form attributable to McNally's skillful appropriations from various dramatic or more broadly literary genres. Taken together, these cover a wide range of possibilities: the social dramas of Anton Chekhov, the psychoanalytically-motivated experiments with interior monologue of Eugene O'Neill in such plays as *Strange Interlude* and *Mourning Becomes Electra*, and an emergent genre on the contemporary stage that Robert Brustein has rather cynically termed "yuppie realism." For Brustein, the conventional formula of this genre, refined by McNally, Richard Greenberg in *Eastern Standard*, and Wendy Wasserstein in *The Heidi Chronicles*, is fairly simple: "romantic comedy with a message, in which the audience is allowed to pay for its entertainment with a dollop of liberal guilt" (28). And it is also Brustein who remarks about the O'Neillian qualities of McNally's play: "And like [*Strange Interlude*], *Lips Together, Teeth Apart* skirts perilously close to sudsy dishwater—a kind of *Strange Interlude* for suburbanites, an infidelity play for the leisure class" (28). Such a comparison, albeit provocative, is also highly misleading. For while the interior monologue O'Neill adapted to reveal psychological nuance is indeed "awkward," it *cannot* function in quite the same expository or corroborative way in McNally's overtly post-Freudian world. In other words, that "yuppie" leisure class Brustein finds so frivolous, and I must admit to some difficulty viewing Sam Truman as a "yuppie," is one or two moments "beyond" Nina Leeds' neuroses and Freud's *Beyond the Pleasure Principle*, which was a major influence on *Strange Interlude*. The fears and troubled subjectivities of McNally's characters, constant topics in *Lips Together*, are irreducible to the "traumatic neuroses" of Nina's past and her enormous sense of guilt (her refusal to consummate her relationship with Gordon Shaw before his death in World War One, for example, and her resultant training as a nurse), some of the lessons O'Neill learned from Freud. Although Brustein is astute in identifying "catastrophes associated with water" as comprising a "central metaphor" of the play—a swimming pool belonging to an AIDS victim, an ocean into which a neighbor purposefully swims in emulation of Norman Main's suicide in *A Star Is Born*—he might also have mentioned the significance of water in Sally's account of her dead brother David's sexuality and in Chloe's story about her skinny-dipping with John on their honeymoon. He might further have identified, as David Richards does, another juxtaposition clarified by the play's final moments: that between a slow, tortuous death symbolized by Sally's brother David struck down by AIDS, and the instantaneous zap of mortality conveyed by the blue light and crackle of the ultraviolet bug lamp. Contrary to McNally's stage directions, which specify that the "main source of light" in the last act emanates from the pool (105), Richards perceived the "eerie blue glow" emitted by the bug catcher as the stage's "predominant light" (146). In fact, the characters are framed at the end by both lights, frozen in tableau until, as McNally's directions indicate, the stage and house lights come up into a final "blazing" climax achieved in consort with a crescendo from Mozart's *Cosi fan tutti*. In sum, the "sudsy" psychological "dishwater" of which Brustein complains is deeper and more streaked with currents than his reading allows.

Taking a different tack, Benilde Montgomery asserts McNally's reliance upon the pastoral tradition in *Lips Together, Teeth Apart*. As he emphasizes, the play is set in an affluent gay community on Fire Island called The Pines, which forms a kind of Arcadia or a "place where it is 'safe to be gay'" located between the "formed civilized" border of New York City and the sea (548). Throughout the play, there also exists a conventional "tension between the visitors from the mainland" (550) and the inhabitants of this Paradisean island ("This is paradise," Chloe tells Sally at the beginning of the play), a tension associated with music, dancing, and the frank expression of homosexual desire. In these ways—in its natural beauty and its blissful remove from the city—the Pines recalls not only the pastoral tradition but also modernism's interest in the primitive and its frequent valorization of natural locales distanced from the stifling, mechanized modern city and its unbearable repressions.

Most significantly, the gay residents of The Pines bask in the refulgence of a fully gratifying sexual life denied McNally's unhappily married couples and partially impotent husbands. In Act One, Chloe tells John of her desire to make "big love," "*l'amour grand*" (46), not a reprise of the blasé lovemaking of the night before, and, as I have mentioned, later describes the *coitus interruptus* of her honeymoon: "Unfortunately, just as you-know-who was getting ready to climax. . .we sort of floated, bobbed ourselves into another couple who were doing exactly the same thing" (58). John, later shaken after his altercation with Sam and given to self-recrimination, admits that the violence he dreams of doing to people who offend his sensibilities emanates from his own sense of impotence to do anything else. Even the momentary spark of Sally's and John's affair is extinguished. By contrast, the loud Fourth of July parties in this gay Arcadia testify to the sexual vitality of the community, something Sam and Sally still cannot quite accept:

Sally: Look they're dancing up there. Both houses.
Sam: That's not all some of them are doing.
Sally: I wish I had a better opinion about all this.
Sam: I know. It's hard. (129)

Here Sam might be taken at his word; after all, he has just watched two men make love and is clearly envious of their passion: "I am watching two men make love in the bushes next to the house. It's probably poison ivy, but they don't care. They are in the throes of passion" (124). In McNally's dramatic worlds—Sally's beach house, Gregory's house by the lake, and even Frankie's apartment awash in the opening act with the release of laughter, the beauty of Debussy's "Clair de Lune," and the spill of moonlight on their desire—passion and the pastoral reside in close proximity to each other.

Lips Together, Teeth Apart, then, resonates with both the bitter-sweet tones of Chekhov and the celebratory trajectory of pastoral; it contains several moments of brooding O'Neillian introspection and, yes, several others of more banal "yuppie realism" (how much to overeat at breakfast and on precisely what delicacies?). And, although none of these hypotheses about dramatic form can illuminate the entire work, each provides at least some minimal purchase on the play. One such critical assertion, however, is considerably less successful in my view: that which attempts to describe McNally as a postmodernist. The dubiousness of the hypothesis may partially explain why some critics seem to retreat from the idea as quickly as they introduce it, Montgomery for example:

Like traditional pastoral, the design of Lips Together, Teeth Apart *allows us to see the ideal world as an alternative to the one in which we must live.* . . . *If, for a modernist imagination like Eliot's, the solution to human isolation was a reintegration of private life with public myths, a* postmodernist like McNally *cannot offer such an easy alternative. (554; my emphasis)*

More mysterious and, finally, more unsatisfying than Montgomery's belated allusion to postmodernism in a reading devoted almost entirely to McNally's indebtedness to pastoral tradition is John DiGaetani's vague ruminations about postmodernism in his introduction to *A Search for a Postmodern Theater: Interviews with Contemporary Playwrights* (1991) and, then, his failure even to broach the topic with McNally in his conversation with him. Is "postmodern" merely a synonym for "contemporary"? Is a postmodernist, using Montgomery's terms, definable as one who refuses to pose an "easy alternative" to complex dilemmas? By now, it must be obvious that I do not regard this critical gesture as adequate, and in the space remaining I would like to re-open the matter of McNally's postmodernist leanings in *Lips Together, Teeth Apart.* Not surprisingly, the body and desire play major parts in this project.

McNally's Postmodernism?

A generation neither fired by ambition nor fueled by the energy of re-pression, but completely refocused upon themselves. . . . "Clean and per-fect." The Yuppies. Their joyous readaptation sings out in their very name. . . . The Yuppies are not defectors from revolt, they are a new race, assured, amnestied, exculpated, moving with ease in the world of performance, mentally indifferent to any objective other than that of change and advertising. . . .

—Jean Baudrillard, America *(1988)*

Brustein's Yuppies and Baudrillard's postmodernism American style—parallels might be drawn between them, all imperfect, yet all useful in reading *Lips Together, Teeth Apart.* Baudrillard's postmodern Ameri-cans and McNally's Islanders are, to begin, as narcissistically obsessed with the body as Ellmann's West Coast cultural critics (Baudrillard terms this a "cult of the body"): both live in a kind of Paradise (Baudrillard denigrates it as "artificial"); both wallow in excess, thus leading to the paradoxical dilemma of worshipping the body while at the same time being "suffocated by plenty," "stocking everything," and inevitably becoming overweight (*America*, 40). Many of these issues surface in *Lips Together, Teeth Apart* as soon as the lights come up on the action. Looking into the pool, Sally seems to echo Baudrillard's characterization of a sanitized America, "It looks clean. It looks immaculate." Right before Sally's lines, Chloe begins the play on a note of postmodern excess and self-indulgence:

Is anyone still hungry? Does anyone want more? I've got eggs, bacon, bagels, Sara Lee, Entenmann's, fresh-squeezed orange juice, coffee, de-caf (Colombian water processed), Special K, English muffins, French muffins, Dutch muffins, German muffins. (5, my emphasis)

The plenitude that Chloe's list reveals, uttered so unambiguously in the play's inaugural lines, might have motivated Brustein's label "yuppie realism"; he never explains its origin. But the matter is fi-nally more interesting than the subtext of Brustein's evaluation. Chloe's list, in which foodstuffs (eggs) and brand names (Sara Lee), plain description ("fresh-squeezed" juice) and the language of adver-tising ("water-processed"), are so imbricated, positions McNally's play within a postmodernist context surveyed by commentators as different as Baudrillard and Edward Bond. Yet, as I have mentioned, this context is not entirely without its own set of problems.

Demonstrating the link between post-Marxian disappointment about the possibility of revolutionary change in contemporary society and the theorization of postmodernity, Bond speculates on the dire implications of what he sees as a displacement of *need* by *wants* in postmodernist culture, what Baudrillard terms "Utopia Achieved." In "the world of needs," Bond contends, "the boundary was always the site of Utopia"; that is to say, "needs were met but Utopia was unobtainable. That was its function." But "wants can have no Utopia—if you are in heaven you cannot have Utopia" (239). As Louis Marin and Fredric Jameson after him also posit, "Utopia" thus possesses a properly *critical* valence; Bond alludes to this capacity as the "grit of hunger, cold, and mortality" implicit in ideas of the Utopian, hence its ability or function to enact a "radical interrogation" of the social (239). Both Bond and Baudrillard, of course, employ the term "Utopia" with a heavy measure of irony; for Bond, "we are in heaven but cannot get out of hell" (237), a hell in part made up of an impossible code of perfection and the ascendance of the image that Baudrillard has spent so much time tracing. Among her other considerable virtues—as entertainer and wit, for example, the only one in this often-funny play who comes close to qualifying for such roles—Chloe also serves as an exemplar of excess and wants: more food, more changes of fashionable ensembles, more sex. Does she really *need* anything so much as she *wants* everything? In a world of Paradisean beauty and conspicuous consumption, as participants in an "orgy of goods and services, an orgy of power and useless energy" (Baudrillard 96), therefore, McNally's Yuppies and Baudrillard's postmodern Americans would seem to have quite a lot in common.

Everything, that is, but the materiality of gendered bodies and sexual desires and that insidious thing called AIDS. Baudrillard's (and to a lesser extent, Bond's) postmodernism defines a hyperreal moment in which simulation has achieved preeminence over the real. In *America*, Baudrillard describes a "perfect definition of the simulacrum" as "*something more real*" than the originary or first performance or object (41); earlier in such works as *Simulations* (1983), *The Ecstasy of Communication* (1987), and *The Evil Demon of Images*

(1987), he outlines the power of the image and its "force of diversion, distortion, capture, and ironic fascination" (*Demon*, 14–15). Images, Baudrillard argues, are never real; rather, they always *appear* "to refer to a real world, to real objects, and to reproduce something which is logically and chronologically anterior to themselves. None of this is true" (*Demon*, 13). Since conformity is the ultimate aim of the image—on this point Bond and Baudrillard would seem to agree—difference, especially gender difference, is under constant attack and potential erosion within postmodern culture. From this initial position, Baudrillard poses a series of questions important, I believe, to a reading of *Lips Together, Teeth Apart:*

[T]his is a culture based on the questioning of one's own definition: "Am I sexed? What sex am I? Ultimately, is sex necessary?" . . . After a triumphalist phase, the assertion of female sexuality has become as fragile as that of male sexuality. This is why there's so much love-making, so many children produced: there at least you still have proof that two people are needed so difference still exists. (America, *46–47)*

From these question, Baudrillard can reflect upon "gender-benders" like Michael Jackson and Boy George and the so-called "'muscle-woman' who, simply by using her vaginal muscles, manages to reproduce the effect of male penetration exactly" (47). Such accomplished, self-referential beings, Baudrillard maintains, can get along without difference.

McNally's week-end vacationers cannot, nor can many of the characters in such plays as *Love! Valour! Compassion!* and *The Lisbon Traviata.* The "difference" is, however, well, different in such plays. Stated in another way, and returning to *Lips Together, Teeth Apart* and Chloe's inexhaustible list of desires, which does she want more: to "take a dildo" to John so he can "see what it feels like" in her fantasy of *l'amour grand* (46) or to imagine him more amply equipped with a penis as "impressive" as her brother's? Understandably reluctant to expose himself upon his sister's request, Sam asks Chloe, "What drugs do you take? What cult have you joined?" (93). But when he relents, Chloe cannot resist mentioning, "It's much bigger than you-know-who's, certainly in that state of flaccidity" (94), exacting some measure of revenge or "payback" she and Sam can enjoy: John and Sally's affair, so painful to both Chloe and her brother, was perhaps not so much *l'amour grand* in at least this single respect. Sam and John's genitals constitute, in fact, a motif in the play. In addition to the instances mentioned above, in Act One, while John announces his erection to Sally, Sam is in the basement decapitating a snake; in Act Three, Sam reads a copy of *Life* magazine and runs across a picture of Portuguese Man-of-Wars, saying to John, "Imagine if those things got wrapped around your dick?" (113). John would "rather not," because, however diminished and impotent he feels, difference still matters.

And so does the body in McNally's plays: Frankie's breasts, Gregory's knees, even James Jeckyll's lesion in *Love! Valour! Compassion!.* No simulations here, as in Baudrillard's Los Angeles; no "digital tongue," "hyperreal penis," and "electric flesh" in McNally's world, as in Arthur Kroker's *Spasm* (1993), a multi-media by-product of Baudrillardian rumination. The "floating body" and "nomadic" tongues of Kroker's virtual reality are much more grounded, much more material in *Lips Together, Teeth Apart* (even though many of McNally's characters might take some interest in Toni Denise, the "recombinant brother," "perfect transsexual woman," "a virtual woman or virtually a woman" with a "male mind colonizing the female body" [26]). Within the discourse of postmodernity, AIDS has in several ways refocussed our attention on the body in its materiality.

How that materiality—and, finally, difference—inflects our understanding of sexual desire is another matter, one Sally in particular ponders in regard to her dead brother David's homosexuality. This brings us back to water, to the pool from which Sally later drinks, and to AIDS. She makes at least this part of the symbology crystal clear:

We all think it's infected. We all think it's polluted. We all think we'll get AIDS and die if we go in. (117)

David and his black lover, after all, have made love in this water that is now death; splashing water on John, Sally urges her friends, "Then let's all get AIDS and die!" (119). Soon, all four of them are wet, damp with love and death, the former of which Brustein fails to recognize in his identification of water's significance in the play. For David's gayness is associated not only with the pool but also with his father's throwing him off a pier when he was four or five years old, expecting him to paddle instinctively back to safety. When David was not capable of swimming on his own, as Sally explains, his father rescued him in a traumatic moment that Chloe, playing the role of psychoanalyst, wants to posit as determinative of David's never having had "a chance" to be "straight" (83). Sally quickly rebuts this hypothesis—"I think the causes of our sexuality run a little deeper and are a hell of a lot more mysterious than being thrown off the pier"—but Chloe persists with her valorization of the psychical importance of the family: "It's entirely the parents' fault" (84). In this confrontation of *modern* explanation with *postmodern* undecidability, McNally seems to side with the latter, as Montgomery suggests.

Indeed, throughout *Lips Together, Teeth Apart*, similar explanatory models are invoked and collapsed, and it is in this respect that the play—and McNally's art—seems most postmodern. Discussing her inability to deliver children, for instance, Sally alludes to the inadequacy of what is largely an Aristotelian conception of causality in explaining her condition: "It's comforting, Sam. It's a story. It has a beginning, a middle, and an end. It has cause and effect, unborn heroes and a villain" (22). The reality of infertility is more complex, less rational. So is the evolution of John's cancer: "I have a cancer, Sally. It's only a little speck now. . .but they tell me it will grow and ripen and flower in this fertile bed of malignancy that has somehow become my body. I never meant it to" (25). Moments later, Sam enters the discourse of the undecidable, the random and catastrophic: "My brain has become a collision course of random thoughts. . . . I'm not sure of anything anymore" (42). Kroker describes such a dilemma in *Spasm*: "All the old certainties dissolve, where everything can finally become uncertain, probablistic, and indeterminate" (33). Freud's emphasis on the family's impact on the psycho-sexual development of the child, Aristotle's delineation of an inherently rational unity of action, liberal-humanist conceptions of a grounded subject—*Lips Together, Teeth Apart* contains adversions to all of these "old certainties," and all of them are exposed as ultimately ineffectual or outmoded. Reality has exceeded or surpassed these traditional explanatory models, leaving only prejudice and conspiracy theory as always already inadequate substitutes for a totalizing discourse to help us face the radically contingent, the indeterminate, the undecidable.

What these passages also suggest, especially in light of the play's beginning, is that while all the characters are analogous in their roles as prodigious consumers (Brustein's yuppies again) and thus in some ways emblematic of the "unparalleled standardization" within postmodernism of which Bond complains so bitterly, their bodies confirm their participation in, or victimization by, a paradoxical "unparalleled rate of change" or mutability they cannot control (Jameson, 15). AIDS has brought this fact home with horrific clarity, and in their own ways Sam, John, and Sally—whatever their anti-gay prejudices—seem finally to come to some understanding of this by the end of the play. Their bodies, like David's, constitute sites of mutability and gradual mutation, the *precise* origins of which they can neither explain, nor control. In this way, perhaps, they stand for all of us as residents of a postmodern world, a world evolved beyond the explanations which have for so many generation provided us with some measure of consolation and reassurance. We may swim or frolic in these explanations, blissfully confident about what interpretive purchases we drink in, but in the background the crackle and blue light of the contingent and catastrophic remain predominant.

At the same time, and irrespective of the formal hybridity of such plays as *Lips Together, Teeth Apart,* the articulation of McNally with postmodernism or postmodernist aesthetics seems fraught with difficulties. The materiality of the body, its beauty and its decline, can never be subsumed by the image or the hyper-reality of the simulation. The body is too textual, too rife for reading—too real. And this reality makes all the difference in McNally's drama, as the body cannot be reduced to a simulation or mere image—or to a theoretical shibboleth. It is too present to be lost in an image, too lost and susceptible to catastrophic change to be positioned securely within totalizing explanation.

Notes

1.   For a discussion of the importance of catastrophe theory to Baudrillard's conception of postmodernism, see my "Baudrillard's America (and Ours?): Image, Virus, Catastrophe."

2.	Because DeBord's *Society of the Spectacle* is numbered by paragraph, not page, citations refer to paragraph number.

Works Cited

Baudrillard, Jean. *America*. Trans. Chris Turner. London: Verso, 1988.
———. *The Evil Demon of Images*. Trans. Paul Patton and Paul Foss. Sydney: The Power Institute of Fine Arts, 1987.
Bond, Edward. "Notes on Post-Modernism." In *Two Post-Modern Plays*. London: Methuen, 1990. 211–44.
Brustein, Robert. "Yuppie Realism, Continued." *The New Republic*, 21 October 1991: 28–29.
DeBord, Guy. *Society of the Spectacle*. Detroit: Black & Red, 1983.
DiGaetani, John L. "Terrence McNally." *A Search for a Postmodern Theater: Interviews with Contemporary Playwrights*. Westport, CT: Greenwood Press, 1991. 219–28.
"Doctors and AIDS." *Newsweek*, 1 July 1991: 48–57.
Ellmann, Maud. *The Hunger Artists: Starving, Writing, and Imprisonment*. Cambridge: Harvard University Press, 1993.
Jameson, Fredric. *The Seeds of Time*. New York: Columbia University Press, 1994.
Jeffords, Susan. *Hard Bodies: Hollywood Masculinity in the Reagan Era*. New Brunswick: Rutgers University Press, 1994.
Kroker, Arthur. *Spasm: Virtual Reality, Android Music and Electric Flesh*. New York: St. Martin's Press, 1993.
McNally, Terrence. *Frankie and Johnny in the Clair de Lune*. Garden City: The Fireside Theatre, 1987.
———. *Lips Together, Teeth Apart*. Garden City: The Fireside Theatre, 1992.
———. *The Lisbon Traviata*. Garden City: The Fireside Theatre, 1990.
———. *Love! Valour! Compassion!* Garden City: The Fireside Theatre, 1995.
Montgomery, Benilde. "*Lips Together, Teeth Apart*: Another Version of Pastoral." *Modern Drama* 36 (1993): 547–55.
Richards, David. "Two Shapes of Comedy—Tragic and Spoof." *New York Times*, 13 July 1991: 145–47.
Watt, Stephen. "Baudrillard's America (and Ours?): Image, Virus, Catastrophe." In *Modernity and Mass Culture*. Eds. James Naremore and Patrick Brantlinger. Bloomington: Indiana University Press, 1991. 135–57.

Chapter Five
McNally's Films of
His Broadway Plays

Helen T. Buttel

Terrence McNally has scripted films for only two of his major plays to date, and both have lost complexity in the translation. Addressing the plays to Broadway audiences, he invents subversive games in order to engage both straights and gays. In *The Ritz* (1975) he introduces three straights from an Italian Mafia family, plus a straight detective and a straight Puerto Rican female nightclub singer, into a seedy gay bathhouse in New York and then lets them dominate the stage, the better to mock their homophobic attitudes and ethnic peccadillos. And he makes one very witty, fast-thinking gay the true hero of the proceedings. In *Frankie and Johnny in the Clair de Lune* (1987), McNally writes what is usually described as a heterosexual romance but is more accurately a naturalistic problem play to which he invites alert spectators, through the gender ambiguity of Frankie's name (Clum, *Acting Gay*, 190), to contemplate the title characters as a working-class man and woman, as scripted, or as two working-class men, either pair trying to find love and tenderness in a hostile world. In each case the film version addresses a less sophisticated audience, glosses over the problems of homosexuals in a straight community, and brightens up the darker implications of the plays.

The Ritz comes close to the carnivalesque, with its marginalized grotesques, gay and straight, seemingly turning ordinary bourgeois life upside down, taking a raucous holiday from the official culture. At its best it is a Dionysian festival, though the debauchery is implicit rather than explicit, and the Lord of Misrule never gains full command. McNally focuses more directly on the invasion of the gay bathhouse by straights, only one of whom knows it is a gay bathhouse, and his reason for being there is to kill his straight brother-in-law, not to fraternize with the gays. They are not there on holiday from conventional rules and restrictions as the gay patrons are; indeed, they are laughably terrified by gay advances, and the play is centered more on farcical mistaken identity problems than on bacchanalia. Two of the gays, Chris and Claude Perkins, do achieve a few mildly Dionysian moments, but the funniest scenes are closer to Feydeau farce than carnival. This is a slight problem for both the play and the film, since they seem to promise more of the carnivalesque than they deliver, or as John Simon complained when the play opened, "McNally's intention is to dabble in religious, ethnic and sexual humor without offending the most middle-class and middlebrow sensibilities"; Simon finds the play "fairly unfunny" because it "tries too hard to remain a clean dirty joke"(65). While the witty dialogue and the farcical stage business do keep the laughter rolling, one cannot help feeling how much stronger both the play and the film could have been if McNally were a freer spirit.

McNally's forte in *The Ritz* is his reflexive playing with performance in the tacky bathhouse nightclub, appropriately called The Pits, where he again comes close to carnival during Amateur Night, toward the end of the play. Nevertheless, it is farce—with its mistaken identities, its jokes and double-takes, its witty repartee, its split-second timing of perfectly choreographed chases and sight-gags, its Punch-and-Judy bopping, its neatly tied-up plotting—which holds the play, and the film, together.

The Art Deco set (by Lawrence King and Michael H. Yeargan in the Broadway production), with its grand split staircase connecting three floors, its many corridors, balconies, and patron's rooms with their beds to dive under and doors to open and slam is the perfect design for director Robert Drivas's splendid choreography of the sight-gags and chase scenes that develop from a proliferation of mistaken identities. These begin with fat Midwestern garbage contractor Gaetano Proclo's arrival at the Ritz, which he mistakes for a flea-bag hotel where everyone is straight. He wears a ludicrously obvious disguise while trying to avoid his Mafioso brother-in-law Carmine Vespucci, out to kill him to fulfill his old man's dying wish. The bath house gays assume Proclo is gay, and one of them, "chubby chaser" Claude Perkins, is endlessly after him, along with Vespucci—up and down that staircase, through the corridors, in and out of Proclo's room, the Steam Room, The Pits. Everyone assumes that detective Michael Brick, hired by Vespucci to find Proclo and catch him in a compromising position with a man in the Ritz, is gay because he has both a glorious physique and a very high voice. All three straights assume that Googie Gomez, tawdry song and dance queen of The Pits, is a transvestite, and Googie mistakes every straight male who enters The Ritz for a producer who will discover her and raise her to stardom, following the model of Bette Midler who became a star after she was discovered in New York's Continental Baths (Murf, 19).

Thanks to McNally's filmscript, most of it transcribed and transposed directly from the play, and his reassembling most of the original cast, the film faithfully records much of this comic horseplay and could have assured a repeat of his Broadway success. But Richard Lester was not the film director to get the most out of *The Ritz*. An American living and directing in Britain, he was the leader of zany exuberance, placing his camera in the midst of the action and ignoring then-current cinematic conventions to introduce a new filmmaking style appropriate to his early sixties Beatles films *A Hard Day's Night* (1964) and *Help!* (1965), his film of Ann Jellicoe's play *The Knack* (1965), and even his film of Steven Sondheim's musical *A Funny Thing Happened on the Way to the Forum* (1966), with Buster Keaton and Zero Mostel, in which he tried to capture filmically the rhythms of the music. But by the seventies he was settling for TV commercials and blockbusters like *The Three Musketeers* (1974) as his once-original fast-cutting, close-up style trickled down into the commercial mainstream. He filmed *The Ritz* at England's Twickenham Studios in twenty-five days (Murf, 19), emphasizing the farce, undermining the nightclub performances and cutting out the serious gay dialogue to finish it off in ninety minutes, a lively, funny, simplified version of the play.

Most destructive to the ensemble farce scenes is the uninspired filmic appropriation of the play's single Art Deco set. Lester uses that Ritz lobby with its grand split staircase, balconies, and corridors for a short establishing shot as Proclo enters at the beginning of the film, but after that he cuts it up, shooting the various bathhouse areas in close-ups and mid-range shots as if for the TV screen. This is just right for double-takes and other reaction shots and for the bopping and diving-under-the-bed routines in the cramped little bedrooms. To capitalize on the large-scale comic ensemble work, however, particularly the choreography and timing of the many chase scenes and extended sight gags, he needed to pull back the camera to frame the action in the full-screen lobby again. The comic elegance of Drivas's ensemble work in the stage production is replaced by Lester's tight, busy shots, which achieve their laughs by cramming each frame with frantic comic action and by such sit-com additions as Proclo climbing into an old Wurlitzer record changer to hide from Vespucci: his head in the glass box looks like a TV talking head swallowing records as Vespucci approaches, noisily shooting his gun.

This is not to say that a better film would merely place the camera in front of the stage and record the play from beginning to end. It is rather that Lester relies almost entirely on the montage approach to filmmaking, telling the story through a series of edited shots. While this approach is ideal for capturing succinctly the high jinks in those small patrons' rooms and for the many sight gags and reaction shots, it robs the film of the play's concentration on performance by neglecting deep-focus long takes of the kind that Charlie Chaplin uses in his long, dance-like sequences where rendering a seamless performance is the only appropriate cinematic object. This technique obviously is more costly than editing close-ups and mid-range shots together, since it increases rehearsal time and numbers of takes. Nevertheless, it is the best way to shoot an ensemble or solo performance when the object is to call attention to the actors performing, not the filmic style.

Lester's montage approach plays particular havoc with the two performances in the Pits which conclude each of the play's two acts. Breaking those numbers down into shots, intercut with shots of actions elsewhere, provides a frenetic sense of Ritz mayhem but none of the satisfaction of watching full-stage run-throughs of the two performances which won the only consistent critical praise for the play. It certainly was not for farce alone that McNally received Achievement in Playwriting citations for *The Ritz* from both the American Academy of Arts and Letters and the National Institute of Arts and Letters (Straub, 457) or that the play ran for a year on Broadway at the Longacre (Murf, 19) after opening at the Yale Repertory Theater as *The Tubs* (Barnes, 377).

But even mutilated by cross-cutting in the film, the reflexivity

of the backstage preparations and the nightclub acts—with attendant burlesquing of theater-people's egos and anxieties as they gird
themselves for the big performance moment—are the centerpiece
of each version of *The Ritz*. Rita Moreno as Googie Gomez, the
Puerto Rican star *manqué* of The Pits, consistently finds the telling
detail that evokes her self-aggrandizement, her anxiety about staying in key with the orchestra, her excessive Puerto Rican accent and
malapropisms as she pursues Proclo, naively mistaking the fat garbage contractor for a producer. Occasionally Lester's added sequences
work to advantage on the screen, as when the camera focuses on a
sign with her name painted on it fastened to a door. The door opens
and as Googie comes out, the sign falls off, revealing the words "Boiler
Room" it covered; she has made herself a star dressing room even in
the scruffy Ritz. With a coy and sheepish look she replaces the sign
and soon propels Proclo into her boiler room-dressing room, the
disjunctive background of her first effort at seducing her "producer."

For Googie's big moment in The Pits, singing and dancing to
"Everything's Coming up Roses," McNally has re-created a real-life
performance which apparently inspired *The Ritz*. In an interview
with Shaun Considine of the *New York Times*, Rita Moreno reported
that at a private theater party for James Coco, attended by McNally
and Robert Drivas, Coco asked her to sing, and she did "Everything's
Coming up Roses," in the style, as she put it, of a "gung-ho Puerto
Rican kid auditioning for the road company of *Gypsy*" (5). A couple
of years later she was performing it every night in McNally's play on
Broadway, getting more rave reviews than any other actor in *The
Ritz*. Moreno, who won an Academy Award for her role in *West Side
Story*, obviously enjoyed parodying an inept singer with the ambition and drive of a real star; every gesture, expression and movement
is deliciously, comically wrong, and at one point in both play and
film she extends a leg so forcefully that her shoe flies off-stage, leaving her to hobble through the rest of the number, singing her heart
out, off-key, and taking breathless, delighted hobbling bows at the
end as if she *were* Bette Midler doing it all perfectly.

Unfortunately, breaking her act down into shots for the film,
too many of them close-ups of her face for this number, and intercutting it with amused reaction shots of Proclo as well as a chase
sequence, undermines her stunningly comic performance and em-

phasizes the farcical chase. At the same time the film does occasionally convey the actors' anxiety about their work and McNally's interest in making theater the subject of his plays. At one point, for example, after Googie has clumsily tossed off her cloak, boa, skirt,
etc., until she is down to a little sequined top and hipsters, the voy-
eur camera circles around behind her to betray her anxiety as her
hand tugs at those tight pants to keep her tush covered while she
sings happily that everything's coming up roses. Also, in the next
Pits performance, Amateur Night, the film makes visible the first
contestant—who is simply heard over a loudspeaker in the play—
singing the Prologue from *Pagliacci*. With a quick insert shot, looking from the stage into the wings, the camera captures two pathetic
costumed singers on the backstage bench waiting to go on, looking
truly miserable. Several shots later one of them stands awkwardly on
the stage with a distressed look on his face, his arms straight forward, then straight up, like a mechanical puppet, singing his *Pagliacci*
bit, badly but gamely.

The prizewinning performance of Amateur Night—Proclo,
Claude Perkins, and Chris in drag, lip-synching, pantomiming, and
jitterbugging to the Andrews Sisters' "The Three Caballeros"—was
on stage a marvel of intricate, well-timed choreography as Vespucci
chases around the fringes of their act and eventually stops it altogether. The film version should have been shot full-screen in one
long take as Googie's "Roses" number should have been, rather than
crosscut with Vespucci's gun-brandishing chase after Proclo. While
Vespucci stops the performance before its conclusion in both play
and film, Lester's incessant intercutting of chases and reaction shots
gives them precedence over the stunning music hall choreography
of "Three Caballeros," in which the two gays have at last got Proclo
into his wife's fur coat. With his long blond wig askew and clownishly lipsticked face, he really gets into the act, a replay of one he did
with Claude during their World War II days in the Philippines,
boogying as if he were one of the gays, though his principal motivation is to avoid his Mafia brother-in-law. In the play this moment
looks more like carnival than anything earlier, straights and gays
together in bacchanalian frenzy. Proclo breaks through his repressions to express spontaneous joy in singing and dancing, despite his
awareness that Vespucci is about to play policeman and stop this

taboo exhibitionism—even as he himself is sought by the police for his Mafia dirty tricks. Once again, however, breaking up this performance by intercutting Vespucci's chase in the film version foregrounds the chase rather than the carnivalesque abandon.

Another poor choice for the film is Lester's intercutting of reaction shots of various gay patrons throughout this number, displaying their delighted identification with the Andrews Sisters act. In the play, the nightclub performances are staged in front of a drop that falls before the Ritz lobby; the actors are thus right up at the front of the stage, performing for the theater audience who may or may not realize they have joined the gay patrons of The Pits when they cheer and applaud. The same effect is often achieved in film by photographing a row or two of audience across the bottom or the side of the screen, with the unbroken performance filling the rest of the space; the movie theater audience then consciously or unconsciously mimics the audience on the screen as they respond to that performance. This camera technique centers on the long take of the performance, yet by including in the shot the border audience of patrons it provides an ongoing view of their reactions at the same time. Andrew Sarris in his review repeated a rumor that Lester never saw *The Ritz* performed and felt this might "explain why so little of the rhythm and raunchiness of the stage production was preserved" (117). To be sure, the film has its pleasures; it is only that McNally's play has more complexity, more concern with the problems and delights of performance life.

You would never think from watching the film version that *The Ritz* is part of a continuum of McNally plays which center reflexively on theater and performance. *The Ritz* shares its burlesque of hopeful theater types, which includes Googie's name-dropping of producers and musicals, with *It's Only a Play* (1986), in which an anxious young playwright, said by John Simon to be McNally parodying himself and his first big Broadway hit *The Ritz*, awaits Frank Rich's review at his opening night party. Simon goes on to observe that with its many references to playwrights, producers, agents, actors, it's "a sort of grand McNally atlas of the theater" (56). David Kaufman said in the *New York Times* that it demonstrates "the indomitable spirit of theater people" (14) as does *The Ritz* play, with its comic focus on the lowliest of theatrical aspirants. Also, the two nightclub performances which get interrupted by the main chase plot of *The Ritz* correspond in their ludicrous way to the Spider Woman's staged performances in McNally's 1993 script for the musical of Manuel Puig's *Kiss of the Spider Woman*. And finally, McNally's inspiration for *Master Class* (1995), like his inspiration for *The Ritz* from seeing Rita Moreno perform at a party, came from observing Maria Callas at Juilliard, advising opera students after her own voice was gone. Amateur Night at the Ritz, with its comic parody of performance, is echoed in the more complex performances of the three opera students, as Googie's absurd self-aggrandizement, her condescending remarks to the Amateurs, her recollection of all the great musicals she has been in echo Callas's more legitimate but nevertheless outrageous ego, her advice to the students, and her reminiscences about her past. McNally's fascination with performance is lost in the translation of *The Ritz* into film, which condescends to the audience when it offers them no more than a farcical TV romp.

The biggest disappointment in the film, however, is the gay bath house. Martin Gottfried, writing about the play, observed that "*The Ritz* could well fortify anti-homosexual, jockstrap heterosexuals. It could possibly insult women (who are treated as ridiculous) and Puerto Ricans and homosexuals most of all . . . if they were awake and could hear above the din" (376). In both play and film—though less pungently in the film—McNally mocks the ethnicity and homophobia of the straight Italians and of Puerto Rican Googie as well and valorizes gay life through Chris, played by young F. Murray Abraham. But he earns critics' negatives partly because he could not or would not control casting, by which both play and film manage to belittle the homosexuals even more than the heterosexual ethnics—without a word of dialogue. The chorus of gay patrons, skulking through the corridors wearing towels, bikinis, boots, cowboy chaps, and hats could have been sexy and flamboyant as they would be in our politically correct present, but instead they are pathetic, sad-eyed, flabby, thin-legged specimens, shy and uncomfortable with newcomers and clumsy with each other. It is as if the directors of both versions deliberately cast actors who by their very appearance and style would inadvertently mock the homosexual role they played, particularly compared to handsome if naive detective Michael Brick or macho if stupid Carmine Vespucci. This typecasting is more problematic in the film than the play, since Lester's close-ups and mid-range shots take us uncomfortably close to the flab, the sad eyes, the thin legs, the awkward mien; on stage, mainly in crowd scenes, these characters are more distanced, less noticeable as individuals. The effect is to give the audience license to ridicule the gays even more than the straights.

Even Chris, the ideal liberated Broadway gay of 1976, unfailingly exuberant in his comic efforts to find a gay partner, wily in his clashes with homophobic Carmine Vespucci, broadminded and humane as he helps Proclo avoid his brother-in-law, is sabotaged by the film. In the play he has a few lines which reveal his disgust with straights like Proclo and Vespucci, as when he tells Proclo that two gay attendants, Tiger and Duff, whom Proclo had assumed were "normal," *are* normal and also have been lovers for three years. He goes on to say that the only thing worth knowing about straight people is that "they don't like gays. They never have. They never will" (27). But he is not the great spokesman for the gays in the film, because it flatly omits this kind of talk. In its place Lester adds some cliché gay stereotyping, such as a shot of Chris, alone on his bed in his rose-lighted, beaded room, arranging a feather boa around his shoulders, primping, and listening to a tape of two men making love.

Altogether, gay life does not look so gay in *The Ritz*. Chris's unrewarded quest for a partner undercuts his joyous exuberance; the patrons are a pathetic group, and straights dominate the stage/screen, even though at the end Chris sees to it that Carmine Vespucci is bound and gagged and dressed in a frilly ball gown before he is taken away by the police. The film's mockery of both gays and ethnic straights too often evokes laughter tinged with malice. The casting of the gay patrons, the fragmented mis-en-scene, and the unvaried cinematic style do a disservice to the film. And on top of that, McNally is too bourgeois to let carnivalesque fantasy take over in this gay bathhouse, to let carefree, low-down joy explode among his assortment of excluded and marginalized people. So he mocks both the straights and the gays for their differences, plays up the farce of mistaken identity and the reflexivity of performance. These will make the play last, if appropriately updated, but the film is at most a frantic, funny, but simplified reminder of what was best about the play.

Clive Barnes remarked that he felt something darker, deeper

and more serious lurking beneath *The Ritz's* "sunny raunchiness," and he'd like to see McNally develop it (377). Very possibly Barnes was responding to the unfulfilled longings of the gays and the homophobic cruelties of the straights already noted. With *Frankie and Johnny in the Clair de Lune* (1987) McNally explores that darkness further, though he masks it with witty dialogue and a hopeful if indeterminate conclusion. In this short, spare two-act play, set in Frankie's one-room apartment during one night—different in every way from the film that followed in 1991—two poor, middle-aged, bright but uneducated people, "not ugly, not beautiful," have just been on their first dinner date. From their bantering conversation—never finishing an idea before starting another and circling back, adding a bit more each time—we learn how much misery this pair who work in the same cafe have known and how little chance they have to escape their pasts. Frankie did not finish high school, and Johnny quit college after two years. Johnny, who has been in jail for forgery, nurtures his self-esteem by quoting literary chestnuts and showing off his advanced vocabulary; he keeps a dictionary and a copy of Shakespeare in his locker.

Their relationship is not easy. At least as dark and bleak as the distance between their dreams and their realities is the continual pattern in their often light and amusing repartee of trying to connect and failing—and, for Johnny, of bouncing back after each of Frankie's defiant rejections. Late in the second act, Frankie reveals what she has been hinting at all along: she had been so badly beaten and abused by one of her boyfriends that she still has a large scar on the side of her head, and she can never have children. As a result, wary Frankie has long preferred living alone to enduring the relationships she invariably falls into. "Why do we get involved with people who it turns out hate us?" Frankie laments. "Because," Johnny begins, but she finishes it, "we hate ourselves. I know. I read the same book" (64). This kind of intimacy and self-awareness might save them, but as soon as they reach a moment of harmony, he overstates his need for her or insults her intelligence, and she retreats—or attacks.

If this sounds like one more forgettable play about the troubled romances of nobodies, the impact of actors Kathy Bates and F. Murray Abraham, succeeded by Kenneth Walsh, and director Paul Benedict in the premier Broadway production helped overcome that problem as does McNally's trademark use of music as a motivating life-force—even for those like Frankie and Johnny without musical training. Most notably, Glenn Gould's version of Bach's "Goldberg Variations" opens the play, along with the sound of the two making love on a darkened stage, and Debussy's "Clair de Lune" brightens the play's climax as well as its conclusion, when they sit together on her bed at sunrise, brushing their teeth, Frankie giving "little gasps of pleasure" at the music.

What really takes the drama beyond its indeterminate love story, however, is McNally's toying with gender and gender-stereotyped characteristics. McNally commented to John Clum that *Frankie and Johnny in the Clair de Lune* is "his most autobiographical play, a response to the loss of dear gay friends to AIDS" (190), and certain critics at the Broadway opening mentioned the air of loss. Frank Rich noted the "end of the world feel" of the James Noone set, and the "blank, Edward Hopperesque solitude of the couples' existence"; he added that it is just possible that McNally has "written the most serious play yet about intimacy in the age of AIDS" (C23). Certainly the play is a richer and darker experience for those who perceive that McNally is exploring a human problem, for both gays and straights—the "difficulty of romantic connection . . . in a post-AIDS, terminally cynical age" as Humm puts it in *Variety* (90). Like *Lips Together, Teeth Apart, Frankie and Johnny* may well be as much about what white hetero- and homosexuals "have in common in an infected, diminished civilization as it is about what sets them apart," as Frank Rich said (183). Or as Frankie put it early in the play, "I don't know about you, but I get so sick and tired of living this way, that we're gonna die from each other, that every so often I just want to act like Saturday night really is a Saturday night, the way they used to be" (21). Nevertheless, AIDS itself, except as it infects the tone, is not so important to the play as the problem of living with difference—male or female, gay or straight.

It is a notable McNally effort to address both groups without parody or malice, to find both gender roles in himself, in all of us. And at its best its oppositions transcend gender. He said of *Frankie and Johnny* in the Introduction to *Three Plays by Terrence McNally*, "I do know I felt I was Johnny while I was writing it. I identified with him completely. . . . About a year later I was watching a production of the play at the Mark Taper Forum in Los Angeles when I realized I was Frankie"(xi). In a *New York Times* pre-opening interview with David Kaufman, he noted that it has been as difficult for him to deal with acceptance of his work as with rejection and to balance his desire to withdraw with his need to be aggressive—the very opposites apparent in Frankie and Johnny. Indeed one begins to realize that like a minor-league Shaw or Stoppard he has constructed in *Frankie and Johnny in the Clair de Lune* a sometimes witty, sometimes vehement dialogue between his opposing selves. As he said in the same interview, "Emotionally all my plays are very autobiographical. A writer doesn't have to experience the events of his plays, but he has to know the feelings" (3). He concludes, again revealing his immersion in both genders, both personality types in this play, "You know I can be too much like a Frankie, but I want to be a Johnny" (14).

The darkness and the dialogue between opposites that pervade the play are barely perceptible in the 1991 film, whose title has been clipped to *Frankie and Johnny* and whose music except for a touch of the Debussy at the end has become appropriately popular. In the Kaufman interview, McNally said the play began for him with an image of Frankie and Johnny, and he did not know where it came from. "Maybe," he added, "it has something to do with getting older, my feeling how fragile life is and how terribly important relationships are. No one dies in *Frankie and Johnny*, but there's this sense of getting on, of making life happen" (14). The play evokes the frustration and pathos of unfulfilled yearning as the two middle-aged nobodies try to make life happen, while the film becomes a demonstration of people connecting. It is as if after probing the darkness of his inner oppositions as openly as he was able in the play, he withdrew to the safety of his usual lighter, comic tone for the film. McNally manages to have it both ways by writing two versions of this story.

As with the filming of *The Ritz*, the choice of director assures a light-hearted, superficial approach to the material. Garry Marshall, known for writing and producing such TV sitcoms as "Mork and Mindy," "Happy Days," and "Laverne and Shirley" and who had just directed the sprightly box-office hit *Pretty Woman* (1990), opens up the spare, single-set play into a sweet, two-hour-long New York love story and counteracts the play's sense of poverty, loneliness, and loss with a montage of pretty pictures, connected by appealing music and sound effects. Even here he is inconsistent. In one instance, during the all-important opening credits sequence, the music inadvertently creates a tonal problem: McNally's title and script emphasize Johnny's pairing of his and Frankie's names as lovers (as Johnny likes to tell her, referring to the first line of the folk song, "we were lovers before we met"). Nevertheless, Marshall puts the whole song on the soundtrack, including not only that Frankie and Johnny were lovers but also that Frankie killed Johnny "cuz he done her wrong"; meanwhile he intercuts images of Frankie's visit to her family in Altoona, Pennsylvania, for a christening and her bus trip back to New York with those of Johnny's last day in the Park View Correctional institution and his bus trip to New York. A spectator who is listening and recognizes crosscutting as the cinematic code for simultaneous action cannot help expecting some meeting, love, and disaster between this pair as they converge on New York. The murder which ends the song never happens in the film, and yet Marshall repeats the whole song at moments when Frankie and Johnny are happy together, thus unintentionally re-introducing a note of foreboding which neither McNally nor Marshall intends.

Frankie's drab, messy one-room apartment has not only become well decorated and tidy for the film but has also lost its place as the story's visual center to the spotless Apollo Cafe in Hell's Kitchen. She and Johnny, along with a lovable group of cooks and waitresses, work there under the guidance of kindly Greek owner Nick who gives Johnny a job right out of jail because he got a second chance himself when he came to America. The story line of the romance as it develops at the Apollo is regularly told in cascades of quick shots, close-up and mid-range, of cooks chopping vegetables, waitresses submitting orders, serving and talking with customers, watching, talking to each other and the new cook Johnny, all evoking their happy social world of work.

These sequences invariably counteract the darker, less frequent montages of the Apollo staff members in their separate apartments, alone and lonely, at night. Particularly telling is a shot of Frankie in the darkness of her room, eating peanut butter out of a jar, watching the people in the apartment across from hers. With her profile along the side of the screen the camera frames what she sees in each window: a prostitute undressing, a man removing his wig, a couple who eat without speaking, a man beating a woman to the floor. In the play, Frankie described the latter two to Johnny; the first two extend the theme of pain and loneliness, but the final shot in the film's sequence, in which a loving older couple play with their dog, counterbalances the bleakness in the upbeat Marshall manner.

Marshall's need to brighten the darkness is apparent even in shots of other locations where these people socialize after hours. A sequence of shots early in the film of the lonely death of the oldest waitress and her funeral (briefly attended by four of her Apollo friends) is counteracted by a sequence at a big Greek-style farewell party for one of the busboys who luckily sold a script to Hollywood; the next montage of shots is of Johnny walking Frankie home through the gloriously blooming flower market at dawn. It ends with a kiss and their first night together in Frankie's apartment. Most of the dialogue from the play occurs after this moment, over half-way through the film, and the idealized images and popular music take precedence over the dialogue—a much-observed film phenomenon—even when the dialogue between the pair is heated. Beauty prevails over their picnic lunch in the park when curt Frankie tells Johnny that he should not assume she was rejecting his advances because she had been messed with as a child but rather because she has been messed with as a woman. And the party spirit cannot be quelled by her anger when he crashes the Apollo waitresses' bowling night. Garry Marshall and music director Marvin Hamlisch make the lunchtime picnic in the park look and sound idyllic, as the pair eat Johnny's gourmet tuna sandwiches, visit bookstalls, play handball together. The bowling alley sequence is also loaded with nostalgia as the camera captures the different bowling styles and abilities of the waitresses, the cheers for Frankie's two strikes (she falls apart when Johnny arrives), and outsider Johnny clownishly bowling with his handball.

As if these changes were not enough to convert a short, spare play into a long, saccharine movie, Marshall gets redundant. Too often characters are actually shown walking from one location to the next when he could have got them there with one cut. In a flurry of overkill, he includes everything as they walk—all the happy street noises, pretty neighborhoods, all the perfectly painted trucks and buses, store fronts, and mailboxes, neatly dressed people of all colors and ages—to evoke a clean, friendly, well-maintained New York City. And it is unnecessary, since he does enough in the substantive scenes to drown us in New York schmaltz. Another kind of redundancy betrays the TV sitcom distrust of spectator reactions: he includes too many shots of characters whose one comment or facial reaction, particularly about Frankie or Johnny, guides viewer response but could have been omitted because it was already implicit in the events of the sequence. In short, this highly edited film needs cutting.

McNally's filmscript makes one positive change in adding a gay character, Tim, and his new lover Bobby to Frankie's apartment building. Tim, an actor, has been Frankie's best friend for years, and their intimacy, unfettered by sexuality, provides a model of what a relationship with another person can be. In a way, Tim is the hero of the film, who beyond advising Frankie about her clothes, her dates, her attitudes, senses Johnny's authentic love for her and in the sisterly intimacy of her bathroom urges Frankie to go to the Apollo farewell party with Johnny, whom he names her "gentleman caller," evoking Tennessee Williams as his guide, as he fusses over Frankie and encourages Johnny's efforts to be open minded about homosexuals. When they leave together for the party, Frankie, in the short, flared, flowered party dress and pumps that Tim has chosen for her (rather than the dark tailored outfit she chose), "Frankie and Johnny" plays on the soundtrack, with its misleading killer-lover motif. Although Tim's relationship with Bobby, briefly sketched, looks about as difficult as Frankie's relationship with Johnny, the scenes between Tim and Frankie, often shot in long takes to reveal the comforting effect of Tim's warm, theatrical nature on withdrawn Frankie, are the sunny center of the film. At the same time the relationship of aggressive Tim and withdrawn Bobby parallels that of aggressive Johnny and withdrawn Frankie, and the conflict between personality types is visualized as a problem for both straight and gay couples. What is implicit in the play with two people is made literal in the film with four. The thoughtful and imaginative participation of the spectator is neither expected nor invited as it is in the play. Hollywood never does trust its audiences to think.

Finally, the casting lightens the tone of the film, inviting the "romantic comedy" label that seemed so inappropriate to the play. Michelle Pfieffer, beautiful even with stringy hair and minimal makeup, and dynamic Al Pacino, each playing against usual type-casting yet glowing in the aura of Hollywood stardom, just cannot transform Frankie and Johnny into the middle-aged losers they were in the play. McNally gives Pacino's character an additional boost in the script: Johnny is not plagued by bouts of impotence as he was in the play but only by forgetting condoms, which Frankie is able to supply, and he does not anger Frankie by asking for a blow-job. Nathan Lane, the charismatic star of many McNally plays—not to mention the film *The Birdcage* and the Broadway revival of *A Funny Thing Happened on the Way to the Forum*—gives Tim his special magnetism. Hector Elizondo, having just played the friendly hotel clerk in *Pretty Woman,* is Nick, the warm, protective owner of the Apollo. Kate Nelligan as love-hungry waitress Cora and Jane Morris as spinster waitress Nedda give their very different comic spins to several scenes at the Apollo and elsewhere, taking their roles well beyond caricature.

The concluding montage is of each of these characters with their appropriate mates in bed in their separate apartments, connected as a family by Debussy's *Clair de Lune* on the sound track. Frankie and Johnny are not sitting on the bed brushing their teeth as in the play but are sleeping spoon in the moonlight. Everyone, aware of how fragile life is and how much relationships help, is connecting. This sweet, slick, well-groomed film, while very different from *The Ritz's* playful farce, shares with the earlier film the encroachment of Hollywood and TV sensibilities; the two films pander to TV notions of popular taste, softening or sentimentalizing the stage versions. Let us hope McNally for his next film will turn to independent film-makers.

Works Cited

Barnes, Clive. "Making the Most of the Ritz Steam Bath." *New York Times,* 21 January 1975, as reprinted in *New York Theater Critics Reviews,* vol. 36 (1975): 377.
Clum, John. *Acting Gay: Male Homosexuality in Modern Drama.* New York: Columbia UP, 1992.

Considine, Shaun. "A Latin from Manhattan Stars at Last." *New York Times,* 30 March
    1975: sec. 2, 1 & 5.
Gottfried, Martin. "Throwing in the Towel." *New York Post,* 21 January 1975, as re-
    printed in *New York Theater Critics Reviews,* vol. 36 (1975): 376.
Humm. "Frankie and Johnny in the Clair de Lune." *Variety,* 11 November 1987: 90.
Kaufman, David. "Frankie and Johnny Are Modern Lovers." *New York Times,* 11 Octo-
    ber 1987: sec. 2, 3 &14.
McNally, Terrence. *Frankie and Johnny in the Clair de Lune.* New York: Plume, 1991.
———. "The Ritz." *The Ritz and Other Plays.* New York: Dodd, Mead, 1976. 2–67.
———. "Introduction." *Three Plays by Terrence McNally.* New York: Plume, 1990.
Murf. "The Ritz." *Variety,* 11 August 1976: 19.
Rich, Frank. "After Sex, What?" *New York Times,* 25 October 1987: C23.
———. "Struggling to Love, but Aware of the Odds." *New York Times,* 26 June, 1991,
    as reprinted in *New York Theater Critics Reviews,* vol. 52 (1991): 183.
Sarris, Andrew. "Putting on The Ritz." *Village Voice,* 23 August 1976: 117
Simon, John. "Bath House Bathos." *New York Magazine,* 3 February 1975: 65.
———. "The Plot Thins." *New York Magazine,* 20 January 1986: 56–57.
Straub, Deborah. "McNally, Terrence." *Contemporary Authors.* New Revision Series,
    vol. 2. Detroit, Michigan: Gale Research Co., 1962–81: 457–58.

Chapter Six
Interview with Nathan Lane

Toby Silverman Zinman

Editor's Note: Nathan Lane, one of the great comic actors of the American stage, talked with me at his apartment in New York on December 9, 1994.

He has performed in many of McNally's plays, including Lips Together, Teeth Apart, The Lisbon Traviata, Bad Habits, *and, for TV,* The Last Mile, *and most recently,* Love! Valour! Compassion!, *which McNally dedicated to Lane, with this epigraph: "Great heart/Great soul/ Great actor/Best friend."*

He is wearing a black turtleneck and black pants—newly slimmed down for his exposure in Love! Valour! Compassion! *as Buzz, a performance unanimously acclaimed. He followed this triumph with a 1996 Tony for Best Performance by a Leading Actor in a Musical* [A Funny Thing Happened on the Way to the Forum] *at the same time that his first leading role in a film,* The Birdcage, *was a huge hit.*

In person, he is surpisingly not "on" but rather soft spoken and straightforward.

TZ: McNally writes for you, and he told me that he felt you always intuited what he wanted in a line, so it's obvious that your work appeals to him. What appeals to you about McNally's plays?

NL: I remember when I first read a review of *Lisbon Traviata* and it sounded like an interesting play. A few years later they were doing a production at the Manhattan Theatre Club, and I was reading the script on the subway and laughing a lot, even though I didn't know anything about opera. I just thought it was very very funny. And then the way the play changes and ends in a murder, it was very very dramatic. What a great piece of writing this is, what a great part. So,

I was surprised they were having so much trouble casting the role. It was really John Tillinger who thought of me—we had just done Jon Robin Baitz's first play—and we hit it off. They were looking for someone older for the part, but I went in and read one scene, and then they called me and told me they wanted me. It's hard to explain, it's like how relationships start. You hit it off—a similar sense of humor, a similar point of view about the world. I like the way he uses language: it's not totally naturalistic, there are long speeches, sometimes people go off on tangents in the middle of a sentence— he likes words, and I like that too. And I just instantly knew how to do his work—I don't know why. It appealed to me and my sense of humor. A character like Mendy in *Lisbon Traviata* is larger than life, and yet he could also be considered almost a stereotypical gay character. It's so well written, so rich, so many layers—so just when you think he's just this silly opera queen, you find out something else about him, and so he's not just a stereotype. McNally always comes up with a surprise or two in writing his characters.

TZ: Do all the McNally characters you've played [Mendy (in *The Lisbon Traviata*), Sam (in *Lips Together, Teeth Apart*), Dr. Pepper (in *Bad Habits*), Buzz (in *Love! Valour! Compassion!*)] have something in common?

NL: They're all looking for love, some kind of romantic love, reaching out to people. Sometimes they're very lonely people—certainly Buzz and Mendy are lonely. One through opera, the other through musical theatre, they survive, pour their obsessions into all of that. Sam is afraid of losing love, he feels they're drifting apart and that troubles him greatly, he's very frightened by that. So, yes, I think there's a search for love in all these characters. There's a loneliness about all of them, even whatisname, Dr. Pepper, is lonely at the end of the play.

TZ: In *Love! Valour! Compassion!* Buzz suddenly shouts to the audience "I could never do this with anyone watching, of course. Even a boyfriend, if I had one, WHICH I DON'T." McNally says you made that line mean more than he knew it meant when he wrote it. That willingness to expose neediness seems all of a piece with those characters.

NL: Yeah, that's true. He [McNally] may not have thought of it in that way, but it's there, in the language. I think in the reading I did something similar to that the first time around, and then, in rehearsal one day, Joe [Mantello] said to me, why don't you do something with that line. So I said all right. So I did. So because that line was funny, the next line was funny, because he says, "I'd be too inhibited." So rather than this self-pitying thing, I'm too shy. I think it's funnier to play it the opposite way from what Buzz says. This is part of our collaboration.

TZ: I saw you in *Laughter on the 23rd Floor*, just before *Love! Valour! Compassion!*, and that is obviously a very different kind of role in a different kind of play. What does a McNally play tap in you, in your talent, in your technique? Part of what he says he so values in your work, is your perfect adherence to the lines.

NL: When someone writes as well as Terrence does, and Neil Simon,—yeah, you owe them that. I think in the theatre, unlike in movies, the writer is the most important person. They take a lot of time with those sentences. Unless you think, well, maybe the rhythm of it—sometimes when you say something out loud, you might suggest something, or improvise a line. With Terrence I certainly feel comfortable doing that. I can improvise in his style.

For instance, in *L!V!C!* when the choreographer is showing them the wounds from his dances, here's this and here's that, and he's pulled his shorts down, and I come in. I kept saying, there's a joke here—I can't just come in and ignore what's going on, it's too funny— but I don't know what it is. Then one night in previews, I came on and I screamed and I said, "I can't leave you kids alone for a second," and that stayed in the play. I feel free to do that, not only because we're friends, but because he knows that it's about making a moment work, it's not out of ego or me wanting to interfere with his writing; it's me wanting to add to the whole thing, to the character. It's very demanding what Terrence writes, it's not easy on actors, he asks a lot of actors—you really have to turn on a dime, its funny one minute and then suddenly you realize something else is going on. Like in the last scene, you come on, start a scene, and then a moment later there's an emotional breakdown. It's very demanding in that way, but very challenging, very exciting, and that's why you want to work with a writer like that, because he asks a lot of you.

In theatre, it's critical to get the language exactly right. Actors learn bad habits in television or film where they don't really care too much about the writer and they don't care if they paraphrase his language or not. Writers like Terrence or Neil Simon—especially Simon— if you add an "and" or a "but"—you don't get it right, you don't get the laugh; it's very important, it's very carefully thought out.

TZ: That "turning on a dime" those sudden shifts, is what McNally says he values most in his own writing, how like life it is. He was telling me about leaving a party in *the* most expensive suit he's ever owned, falling down because some stairs were invisible in the dark, and tearing it as well as hurting himself. Nothing as he was walking along, he said, prepared him for that sudden moment—and that's what he wants to catch in those shifts. How, as an actor, do you make those shifts work, seem fresh time after time?

NL: Well, you prepare, the way I always do, but to a certain degree it's about what happens when you go out , and I [as Buzz] talk to Stephen [Spinella]—our connection, too. It helps to get yourself in a certain frame of mind—there are certain things I think about, so I know that my emotions are sort of "there"—it's sort of like checking your voice if you're a singer [he sings a brief operatic note], and you know, okay, it's there. I think about where the character is, but there are personal things I draw upon—and then you hope for the best. That's the challenge—doing a show like this eight times a week—I'd like to think that nine times out of ten I get where I want to be emotionally, but sometimes your mind gets in the way or you start looking at yourself as you're doing a scene, or someone starts coughing in the middle and you're distracted. But then I don't fake it; it's just not as emotionally full as you want it to be. It still works for an audience, but for me as an actor . . . I'm very hard on myself. If I can't make that scene work—they're all crying now—reduce them to tears—yes, it's working—then I feel I've failed in some way. My own neurotic thing.

TZ: McNally and I have been talking about opera, since he's about to open *Master Class* in Philadelphia, and he said he thought *Lips Together* was his most operatic play. Did it feel like that to you? that you'd been given language that worked like arias or duets?

NL: It's very operatic, very musical, and because it's just four people, that's why it opens with the quartet from *Cosi fan tutte*. And there are all these inner monologues we share with the audience. When we were rehearsing, I didn't always feel comfortable with them— some of them were easy, just an aside, but sometimes you would have a particularly long monologue. It was demanding because it was written not so much in Sam's voice, but in the author's voice— suddenly he was using words, and I would say, "Sam wouldn't talk like this," but Terrence wanted it to sound a certain way and not the way this person would sound publicly. So it was hard. This *[L!V!C!]* was a much easier rehearsal process—that *[Lips]* was a difficult rehearsal process—we didn't have much time, and when we went into rehearsal, the script was not in strong shape. He had to totally rewrite the first act. It was a hard play to make work—it was three acts—now I'm used to three acts—but then it seemed an enormous undertaking, and there didn't seem to be enough time. I remember Swoozie [Kurtz] saying, I think we should cancel the whole thing, I don't think we're ever going to be ready to do this in front of people. There were a lot of tantrums and fits, a lot of yelling and screaming, but somehow it all came together.

In *Love! Valour! Compassion!* I think he went through several drafts before we got into rehearsal. It was because he had done two readings of it, and he'd been working with Jerry Zaks who might have directed it, so by the time we went into rehearsal it was in pretty good shape. It was still long, but essentially, the shape of it was there.

TZ: During one of the curtain talks, someone asked you if this *[L!V!C!]* was an AIDS play. My impression from your reply is that you felt very strongly that this was a passionate AIDS play.

NL: I don't think it's "an AIDS play" although AIDS is a big part of it—especially my character—but I don't think I would say it was an AIDS play. It's about these gay men, some of whom are dealing with

AIDS, but like any great piece of writing by the end it becomes very universal. Hopefully, if we've done our job well, people won't still be thinking, it's a gay play, it's an AIDS play, but about a group of people who are trying to struggle through life who have formed a family.

Chapter Seven
Where We Are Now:
Love! Valour! Compassion!
and Contemporary Gay Drama

John M. Clum

I.

John: No one cares what you think as a gay man, duck. That wasn't the question. What do you think as a member of the human race?"

In *Love! Valour! Compassion!*, the bitter John Jeckyll poses this question to his weekend date, a young Latino who defines himself both as a person of color and as a gay man. John's question crystallizes a problem for contemporary American drama, which is dominated right now by what are called, for want of a better term, "gay plays." What I shall essay here is a reading of *Love! Valour! Compassion!* which defines what a gay play is at this moment in American social and cultural history.

Being an urban art form, what is left of theater in contemporary society depends on those people left in the city who have an investment in theater as a cultural form and a medium of communication and political engagement. Gay men are one such group. Ignored for the most part by film and television, we turn to drama as a medium which will valorize us by showing us complex, non-stereotypical pictures of ourselves. Broadway gay drama, a small segment of gay drama if still, only mythically, the most important drama produced in America, limits its audience by the ridiculously high price of tickets and the general unpleasantness of attending the user-unfriendly Broadway theaters, devoid of amenities or social spaces. Eventually plays which are successes on Broadway will filter down to smaller, less expensive theaters which have younger, less affluent, more adventurous audiences. But most important gay drama and theater actually is born in such spaces (*Angels in America* began not at the Walter Kerr Theater but at the small, adventurous Eureka

Theater in San Francisco). A gay Broadway play can only speak to those who can afford it and who see going to a Broadway play as an attractive enterprise.

Terrence McNally is in the dubious position of being our most established gay playwright. He has for years been house playwright for the Manhattan Theater Club, one of New York's most prestigious and well-heeled non-profit producing organizations. Unlike the New York Public Theater, the Manhattan Theater Club has never earned a reputation as a multi-cultural "people's theater"—its audience is older, rich, and mostly straight. Yet, McNally built his—and the Manhattan Theatre Club's—reputation with uncompromisingly gay plays like *The Lisbon Traviata* and the American's theater's most probing satire on homophobia, *Lips Together, Teeth Apart.* Long before the critical success of *Angels in America* (which did not make a profit in its needlessly spectacular Broadway production), McNally has been our pioneering Broadway gay playwright. While few of his works began their lives on Broadway, works like the critically scorned *And Things That Go Bump in the Night* (1963), and the gay sex farce *The Ritz* (1974), offered Broadway unabashed views of gay experience at a time when most gay plays were produced safely Off-Broadway.[1] The ecstatic reviews of *Love! Valour! Compassion!* and a special contract with the theatrical unions made a transfer from the Manhattan Theater Club possible. McNally's most recent depiction of gay life earned even more accolades during its Broadway run.

For a long time, it was virtually impossible for a gay play to achieve such acclaim from New York critics. In the sixties, Tennessee Williams, Edward Albee, and William Inge were the objects of vicious homophobic attacks from the New York critical establishment. If they wrote about homosexuality, they were breaking a carefully policed taboo. If they wrote about women they were attacked for writing male characters in drag. Terms like the "Albertine strategy" and "homosexual spite" were bandied about carelessly.[2] Even now, one sees survivors of the sixties critical establishment like Robert Brustein writing a very thinly veiled homophobic review of *Love! Valour! Compassion!*, ironically for the *New Republic,* which is edited by an openly gay man. Brustein denies the play any substance and sees only sexual machination, a minor element in the play's action: "the play has no subject other than sexual relationships—who is sleeping with whom, and how the who and the whom can be arranged" (Brustein, 31). Either the Mandarin of American theater is becoming a bit less sentient or he has imprinted on McNally's play the generic gay play homophobic reviewers find necessary to disdain, "Almost everyone in the play breathes the helium of high camp" (Brustein, 31); actually one character celebrates relatively low camp and the rest are relatively campless. Brustein also sees the gay audience members' appreciation of the play as "a lot of complacent consensual recognition between the spectators and the stage" (Brustein, 31). Take away Brustein's disdainful characterization of the audience—"complacent"—and you have a description of a successful theatrical experience. Brustein's review is a reminder that there is still homophobia among the old guard of the critical establishment as there is among producers and audience members.

John Jeckyll's question, quoted in the epigraph, sums up the problem for a gay playwright writing for a commercial theater audience. Who does care what a gay man thinks? Who other than gay men? And when is a play compromising too much in order to placate the heterosexuals in the audience? Even McNally pandered to the prejudices of a Broadway audience with his perversion of Manuel Puig's novel, *Kiss of the Spider Woman*.

McNally has written that, "I think I wanted to write about what it's like to be a gay man at this particular moment in our history" (McNally, 1995, xii). In doing so in *Love! Valour! Compassion!*, McNally has written a play that is in conversation with the major works of gay drama of the last three decades. It is this conversation that will be the focus of this essay. McNally's play is characteristically courageous in confronting straight audience members with the aspects of homosexuality they may find most unsettling or threatening. My primary interest, however, is on what he shows his gay audience.

As I write this, *Love! Valour! Compassion!* occupies the Walter Kerr Theater in New York, which was previously occupied by Tony Kushner's *Angels in America*. For those with no interest in theater history, this factoid is irrelevant. Perhaps, however, it is a good starting point for any discussion of the place of McNally's estimable play in a picture of where and what gay drama is now.

Kushner's seven-hour extravaganza ended with an odd counter-cultural quartet onstage. A former drag queen living with AIDS; another African-American ex-drag queen, now nurse; a feckless gay Jewish man who talks the politically correct talk but barely acts at all; and a Mormon matron who, having lost her son and daughter-in-law (who have disappeared), takes care of the person with AIDS. Even more interesting is who is not on stage—the only character in the seven-hour play who goes through a real dramatic conflict and crisis, the conservative Mormon lawyer, Joe Pitt, who is thrown into a tailspin by his coming out. Joe represents a lot of gay men who have been brought up with a set of religious and social beliefs which he finds difficult to reconcile with his newly acknowledged homosexuality. Kushner drops Joe off the face of the earth shortly before the end of *Perestroika,* as if he were unredeemable or simply not very interesting. Blond, blue-eyed Joe Pitt, described disdainfully by one character as "the Ken doll," is, like Edward Albee's Nick, a representative of what is wrong with society and conventional American masculinity to be dismissed at the final curtain.

Joe's wife, Harper, tells him to "Get lost," and we are to believe he does. Perhaps if or when Joe loses the baggage of his conservatism, his wish for social order, he can be redeemed and join the elect at Bethesda Fountain where the play ends. Joe's capacity for love, his complexity, his wish, however misdirected, for a redeemed and redemptive society count for nothing in Kushner's scheme.

Yet as I think about *Angels in America,* Joe is the character I care about, anguish over. He is the character who cares about combining his homosexuality with the important elements of human experience, straight or gay, that are left out of Kushner's vision of America: loving, committed relationships; meaningful work; and a constructive politics. Is it possible to be gay and not be counter-cultural? Is it morally wrong to be gay and conservative? Joe is not a monster like the play's archenemy, the homophobic, anti-Semitic gay Jew, Roy Cohn: Joe is capable of love and he is on the verge of coming out. Indeed it could be said that rather than help Joe Pitt out of the closet, the other characters—Louis, Roy Cohn, and Prior, drive him back in.

Kushner privileges Prior Walter, the ex-drag queen living with AIDS, but what does Prior represent except a particularly endearing representative of the fashionable but dangerous Cult of the Victim?

His best scenes in the play are the comic ones in *Perestroika* where he plays a kind of queer Lucy to Belize's Ethel. Only AIDS gives Prior the right to the moral superiority Kushner claims for him.

The basic difference between *Angels in America* and *Love! Valour! Compassion!* is that the former purports to be a queer play while the latter is definitely a gay play. To understand the distinction, one must understand the different political ramifications of the words "queer" and "gay."

In my book, *Acting Gay*, I tried to define historically the changing characteristics of gay drama, a   task that has become more difficult as a distinction is made between "queer" and "gay." While "gay" signifies a male who desires someone of his own sex, "queer" has more complex, more politically charged connotations: a reveling in difference, a belief in performativity over stable essence, a celebration of marginality. In its most radical, Queer Nation definition, according to Alexander Doty, "queer" "means to be politically radical and 'in-your-face:' to paradoxically demand recognition by straight culture while rejecting this culture. Part of what is being rejected here are attempts to contain people through labeling, so 'queer' is touted as an inclusive, but not exclusive category, unlike 'straight,' 'gay,' 'lesbian,' 'bisexual'" (Doty, xiv). For Eve Kosofsky Sedgwick, "queer" is a word that includes all who demonstrate by their claims and action that definitions of sexual identity are fluid, unstable:

That's one of the things that "queer" can refer to: The open mesh of possibilities, gaps, overlaps, dissonances and resonances, lapses and excesses of meaning when the constituent elements of anyone's gender, of anyone's sexuality aren't made (or can't be made) to signify monolithically. (Sedgwick, 8).

"Queer" shows both the failure and the power of hegemonic discourse. It covers what there are no nice words for, because it is an umbrella for proscribed sexual acts, roles, and orientations. More important, for Sedgwick "queer" is a speech act as well as a definition:

But "gay" and "lesbian" still present themselves (however delusively) as objective, empirical categories governed by empirical rules of evidence (however contested). "Queer" seems to hinge much more radically and explicitly on a person's undertaking particular, performative acts of experimental self-perception and filiation. A hypothesis worth making explicit: that there are important senses in which "queer" can signify only when attached to the first person. *(Sedgwick, 9)*

"He's a queer" is an insult, like "he's a faggot," for it places the object inside negative discourse, hate speech. "I'm a queer," says "I am not like you and I do not accept the systems on which you might base a negative judgment of me." Queer, then, is a matter of politics and style. One can be gay without being queer.

This sort of queerness underlies Tony Kushner's *Angels in America*. We are to identify with Louis Ironson because of his marginality. "He could have been a contender," to paraphrase Budd Schulberg, but instead of being a lawyer, he is a word processor; instead of being a devoted lover to his ailing partner, he is feckless. Louis is brilliant, well read, even theoretically sophisticated—he sounds like my graduate students—but he would drop out along the way and fester over his failure. But we are not to lament over wasted potential. There is Louis at the end, still loved by the man he betrayed, along with the queer, as opposed to gay, Prior and Belize, and the potentially lesbian Hannah Pitt. In Kushner's vision, queerness is valorized, but it is also ineffectual. To paraphrase Faulkner, queers endure, but they do not prevail. They are wise enough to know that "The world spins only forward"—that motion is inexorable but not linear and that any form of conservatism that tries to stop the motion is doomed to fail—sometime. But for all the talk about politics, *Angels in America* does not call for political action. You're OK as long as you don't think like a conservative, but in Kushner's America profession, middle-class aspiration and conservatism are equated.

There are more politically consistent "queer" plays and theater pieces than *Angels in America,* but they certainly are not Broadway fare. They are the stock and trade of a more radical gay drama and performance art: from the plays of Robert Patrick, Doric Wilson and the late Robert Chesley to the performance art of Tim Miller. But *Angels in America* manages to be queer without offending the sensibilities of those well heeled enough to pay the $130 it took to see the entire play on Broadway. At the end, instead of attacking the audience, the queer blesses them.

"Gay," like "queer," has taken on specific political connotations, Even if Kushner allowed Joe Pitt a reformation, he would at best become an upper-middle-class *gay* man—a successful lawyer cautiously out in his everyday life but living in a domestic partnership with a socially compatible lover, perhaps belonging to a church with a lesbian and gay group (what is now known as a "welcoming congregation"). He would read Bruce Bawer's *A Place at the Table.* He might subscribe to *The Advocate* and *Out*[3] magazine as well as *The New Republic.* And he would go to Broadway to see *Angels in America* and *Love! Valour! Compassion!.* He might even make it through *Kiss of the Spider Woman* without gagging. Joe Pitt would be gay, not queer. He would acknowledge his sexual orientation, believe that it should be socially acceptable as long as it fit within certain parameters but would want to assimilate into American society. Indeed assimilation would be at the heart of his politics.

I do not present this picture to denigrate it. My sympathies are more with this Joe Pitt than they are with Louis Ironson. Yet Joe Pitt raises some of the most contentious questions for gay men: whether a mainstream politics can or should gel with gayness, which is an offshoot of the larger debate over the extent to which gay men should uncritically accept their patriarchal privileges as men. As Leo Bersani so cogently points out, "Gay men are an oppressed group not only sexually drawn to the power-holding sex, but belonging to it themselves" (Bersani, 66). Gay Joe Pitt, unquestioning still of the fact that his power and conformity have placed him in a morally untenable position, does not deserve to sit with the independent woman, person with AIDS, African American queen, and left-wing intellectual.

Gay drama tends to be about the gay bourgeoisie and tends, as mainstream drama does, to accept middle-class ideals and aspirations even as it may critique some of them. Everyone is allowed a place in the finale of *Love! Valour! Compassion!:* lawyer and accountant as well as costume designer and choreographer. While the end of *Angels in America* essentially celebrates the individual, the ending of McNally's play celebrates the group.

Even the artists depicted in *Love! Valour! Compassion!* do not create "queer" work. There are no Tim Millers invited to this country house. Indeed the commonality of the play for its straight audience is the shared bourgeois status of characters and audience members. We are told that the lawyer and accountant like to play rough in bed, but they do not wear leather and nipple rings. They do not display their difference.

So there is a definite difference between queer theater and gay theater, in essence defined by the difference between the valorization of marginality and the partial acceptance of some basic aspects of American culture. Gay drama is less interested in radical change than in staking a claim for gay people within a more compassionate, open society. Leo Bersani sees the negative aspect of this sort of gayness:

We want to be recognized, but not as homosexuals (the essentialist identity). It is doubtful that we will be mistaken for other oppressed groups by the dominant culture (which is, for obvious reasons, concerned with questions of identity): we may, however, easily be mistaken for the dominant culture. (Bersani, 68)

Or, for assimilationist gays, we may too easily believe that we hold a safe place in the dominant culture, forgetting that a lot of people do not want us there, particularly not wanting us to live too comfortably like them, for that would make a bold statement that homosexuality is an attractive option and compulsory heterosexuality is not necessary and necessarily right. I would suggest, however, that the end of *Angels in America* is more comfortable to a homophobic middle-class audience member than the end of *Love! Valour! Compassion!* The reaching out for blessing from a marginal, relatively unthreatening position is easier to accept than the idealized community of relatively happy, prosperous naked men we see in the latter play.

II.

I know. I'm butch. One of the lucky ones. I can catch a ball. I genuinely like both my parents. I hate opera. I don't know why I bother being gay.

This characteristic bit of humorous self-deprecation is spoken by

Arthur, a gay accountant who has been in a relationship with Perry, a lawyer, for fourteen years. Arthur and Perry represent an upper-middle-class gay marriage. Two solid professions, a nice home filled with all the necessary and unnecessary appliances and electronics coveted by us members of the American bourgeoisie, and a state-of-the-art car for their weekend trips. Arthur and Perry do good works. They contribute to charities, work for AIDS groups, and do *pro bono* work for arts organizations. They are good, solid citizens. Arthur and Perry would never be invited to join the gathering at Bethesda Fountain at the end of *Angels in America*. Not only do they represent the white bourgeoisie Kushner mistrusts, they are also politically and socially conservative. When one of their party starts talking about a newspaper photograph of a starving Somalian child, Perry rejoins:

I think the point is that we're all sitting around here talking about something, pretending to care. . . . when the truth is there's nothing we can do about it. It would hurt too much to really care. You wouldn't have a stomachache, you'd be dead from the dry heaves from throwing your guts up for the rest of your life. That kid is a picture in a newspaper who makes us feel bad for having it so good. But feed him, brush him off and in ten years he's just another nigger to scare the shit out of us. Apologies tendered, but that's how I see it. (52)

Though his lover and friends are appalled at the callousness and political incorrectness of Perry's statement, they share his fear of a world in which everything seems threatening and nothing works properly. Later, when they are alone, Perry tells Arthur: "I hated what I said at the table. . . . I just get so frightened sometimes, so angry." Arthur reassures him that "we all do" (60–61). When Bobby arrives, he tells his lover, Gregory, how things are at their city home: "The city is awful. You can't breathe. They still haven't fixed the dryer" (37). Perry's fear and anger is one way of responding to chaos. Buzz, the ultimate Musical Comedy Queen, has another:

You may wonder why I fill my head with such trivial-seeming information [data about arcane musicals]. First of all, it isn't trivial to me, and second, I can contain the world of the Broadway musical. Get my hands around it, so to speak. Be the master of one little universe. (25)

A sense of order, of control is crucial to these gay men of the 1990s. They suffer from the usual fears of our age plus those particular fears of gay men, painfully aware of their place in American society: "They hate us. They fucking hate us. They've always hated us. It never ends, the fucking hatred" (107). And they are either living with AIDS or with the fear and survivor guilt AIDS inspires. HIV-negative Arthur tells his lover: "I will always feel like a bystander at the genocide of who we are" (122).

The eight men in *Love! Valour! Compassion!* are all prosperous, relatively apolitical, artists or supporters of the arts. In one sense, they could be, and have been, seen as stereotypes, the nineties version of the eight men who gather in Mart Crowley's *The Boys in the Band.* Indeed, McNally seems consciously to be placing his characters within a framework of canonical gay drama. We are told in Act II that "We would have a fabulous 5th of July," an allusion to Lanford Wilson's 1978 play about a gay couple in middle America. Even the casting—Stephen Bogardus (*Falsettos*), Nathan Lane (*The Lisbon Traviata*), and Stephen Spinella (*Angels in America*)—reinforces the referentiality. In one sense, the play, like Kevin Elyot's 1994 London hit, *My Night with Reg,* is a kind of State of the Union for one group of gay men.[4]

Like *Fifth of July, Love! Valour! Compassion!* takes place in and around a beautiful old country house. Here a group of old friends spend their summer holiday weekends. What the six middle-aged men share is a sense of their own mortality. Does that mean something different for gay men than it does for straights? In *Lips Together, Teeth Apart,* John, a heterosexual version of bitter John, the evil twin in *Love! Valour! Compassion!,* has discovered that he is dying of cancer as he is riddled with the feelings of inadequacy and self-hatred that are devouring all the characters in the play:

With or without cancer, I'm still the same person, so there's no reason to change your opinion of me. I mean, riddled with the stuff, I'm still going to be the same rotten son of a bitch. I wish I could change. I really, really, really do. Profoundly. I can't. I just can't. I apologize to all of you. (97)

Lips Together, Teeth Apart takes place in the gay section of Fire Island on a July 4th weekend. The two married couples in the play feel profoundly out of place in a gay ghetto, in a house left to one of the characters by the gay brother she never approved of (he has committed suicide rather than suffer further from AIDS-related infections). The sadness of this play is built on the heterosexuals' refusal to see their commonality with the gay men surrounding them; that their fears, particularly of mortality, are the same. John is right when he says: "Not everyone is dying of AIDS, Sally. There are other malevolent forces at work on God's miraculous planet" (83) but that should not preclude joining with their gay neighbors on the most American of holidays.

For McNally, there are both physical and spiritual malevolent forces. There is the mortality we all must deal with—aging and the loss of feeling desirable without the attendant loss of desire and the horrid diseases particularly ravaging gay men. How does one cope gracefully with these? Also, for those like John, there is the curse of feeling unloving and unlovable, of being evil. Both Johns suggest that mean-spiritedness may also be an incurable disease which lodges in certain people and is as virulent as cancer and the HIV virus. John Jeckyll tells his good twin, James:

I resent you. I resent everything about you. You had Mum and Dad's unconditional love and now you have the world's. How can I not envy that? I wish I could say it's because you're so much better looking than me. No, the real pain is that it's something so much harder to bear. You got the good soul. I got the bad one. Think about leaving me yours. (124)

Unlike Kushner's evil genius, Roy Cohn, who exults to the last in his splenetic displays of malevolence, McNally's bad souls are pained at their own isolation. Yet John Jeckyll is not nasty because he is homosexual. This is not a repeat of the "Oh, God, why am I such a miserable nasty fairy?" refrain of *The Boys in the Band*. McNally's alternation of plays about homosexuals and heterosexuals shows that poverty of the spirit, lack of compassion, are human traits, which in heterosexuals are most dramatically seen in their hatred or fear of homosexuals.

While McNally seems to be suggesting that *Love! Valour! Compassion!* can be seen as a new look at the sort of group Mart Crowley presented in *The Boys in the Band*, one can see by reading the work in the context of McNally's other works, that homosexuality does not define personality here. Yet, as in Crowley's play, there is an attempt in *Love! Valour! Compassion!* to present as much of a cross-section of New York gay society as would credibly be invited to Gregory's house. Arthur and Perry can be seen as the nineties version of Crowley's "straight acting" couple, Larry and Hank, but while Larry and Hank fight to forge a relationship that offers space for sexual freedom, Arthur and Perry see infidelity as a threat and a betrayal. Buzz and James are the resident queens, like Emory and Harold in *The Boys in the Band*, but they also become a loving couple. The beautiful Ramon might be a sex object, like Crowley's cowboy, but he disdains that role and is actually a successful artist. McNally's characters are functioning professionals capable of love. Their homosexuality does not cripple them.

III.

"Desire is a terrible thing. I'm sorry we're not young anymore."

Arthur's melancholy confession to his partner of his attraction to Gregory's beautiful young lover, Bobby, sums up a crucial theme in McNally's play. Tennessee Williams's Blanche DuBois exclaims, "The opposite of death is desire," but what happens to desire as one grows older? For gay men, whose gayness has been tied to their sexuality and sexual attractiveness, this is particularly a problem. The evil genius, John, brings to this country gathering a beautiful, young Puerto Rican dancer who exults in his beauty and his independence. Ramon's physical beauty has a potent effect on all the men. It has also had an effect on the play's audiences and critics as column inches have been spent discussing the physical attributes of the actor who plays Ramon and who spends much of the play nude. That nudity is not a cynical showbiz ploy. Ramon's body is a reminder to these men of what they feel they are losing. John sees Ramon only as a sex object, a male bimbo. Gregory, a dancer-choreographer who is painfully aware that his body will no longer allow him to dance, realizes that he must let the talented Ramon dance his work for him: "Gregory was suddenly a 43 year old man whose body had begun to quit in places he'd never dreamed of, looking at a 22 year old dancer who had his whole career ahead of him" (127–28). When Gregory's lover, the beautiful, young, blind Bobby compromises his relationship with Gregory by having sex with Ramon, Ramon blatantly tells Gregory what his presence has already made clear: "You're old and you're scared and you don't know what to do about it" (118). Bobby, we discover, eventually leaves him because of his age. When Gregory no longer has the physical strength of youth, he ceases being attractive to Bobby.

Despite his love for Perry, Arthur becomes infatuated with Ramon as he has been with the sweet, young Bobby. Arthur knows, however, that he is not attractive to these young men, however much Ramon may flirt and tease, as he knows what cheating can do to a relationship: " . . . it's never been the same. It's terrific, but it's not the same" (19).

John Jeckyll, who has brought Ramon to the country house, tries to relive with Ramon his first adolescent sexual experience, one which involved no actual physical contact. But the story allows John a kind of eternal youth: "He will always be 17 years old and I will always be 19. Neither of us grows old in this story" (95). John cannot regain his youth with his memory anymore than he can with Ramon.

Ramon has the self-confidence and independence that comes with youth and beauty. When asked when he loves himself, he answers:

I love myself when I'm making love with a really hot man. I love myself when I'm eating really good food. I love myself when I'm swimming naked. . . . But most of all I love myself when I'm dancing well and no one can touch me. (55)

Ramon's open sensuality sets him apart from the older characters and links him with Bobby with whom he has a passionate brief encounter in the kitchen. The wild card for all the characters is sexual desire, but the older men opt for order and stability in their sex lives.

At the tense first dinner on Memorial Day weekend, Ramon has the naiveté to spout a truism which, as usual, happens to be true, however trite:

Ramon: *I think the problem begins right here, the way we relate to one another as gay men.*

John: This is tired, Ramon, very tired.
Ramon: I don't think it is. We don't love one another because we don't
    love ourselves. (54)

His could be a line out of *The Boys in the Band*, but McNally's characters are not the self-flagellants of Crowley's play. These men are
functional, even successful. They may not be as self-loving as Ramon,
but there is no doubt of their wish and capacity for love. *Lips Together, Teeth Apart* and *A Perfect Ganesh* showed that McNally believes that self-loathing is an American problem, not a gay one. These
men know their limitations and try to reach out to others construc-
tively.

    The self-hating boys in the band came together because they
were gay and, therefore, misfits. They had nowhere else to go. The
support they offered each other was at best tenuous. McNally's characters have forged a gay family:

*I want to write about family. To me a very important line is when Gregory
says, "Are you going home to Texas?" Bobby says, "No, home is here. Texas
is where my parents are." Gay people do create a society for themselves, an
extended family. And when he says, "Will you be there? Will you promise
me?" that's a very strong reality for a gay person. It may not be to someone
who has a wife or a husband and six children. (Rosen, 21–22)*

This is a major difference between *Love! Valour! Compassion!* and
Mart Crowley's 1968 play, *The Boys in the Band.* In Crowley's play,
eight homosexuals come together for a social event, but one never
understands what, besides their homosexuality, brings them to
Michael's apartment to be vilified. The group may represent Crowley's
idea of a microcosm, but it does not represent a community—or
Crowley is dramatizing his notion that a gay community is impossible. Lanford Wilson's *Fifth of July* ultimately places its gay couple
at the center of an extended biological family but outside any sup-
portive gay community. For all their occasional squabbles, the men
in McNally's play have over a number of years forged strong bonds.

    Though some characters are happily coupled for various lengths
of time, the most important bond is friendship:

Perry: No one for miles and miles. We could be the last eight people on earth.

Buzz: That's a frightening thought.

Perry: Not if you're with the right eight people. (88)

These men form a family with all the attendant stresses and strains. McNally sees the characters in *Love! Valour! Compassion!* as "an extended family with relatives you like more than others" (Rosen, 21). Such assertions raise the central question for gay men: how do we place ourselves within the discourse of family? By retaining or reforging links with our own families if those families have not rejected us. By forging our own intentional families, closely bound communities offering love, support, sometimes patronage. In her fine study, *Families We Choose: Lesbians, Gays, Kinship*, Kath Weston describes gay families she has known:

In the Bay Area, families we choose resembled networks in the sense that they could cross household lines, and both were based on ties that radiated outward from individuals like spokes on a wheel. However, gay families differed from networks to the extent that they quite consciously incorporated symbolic demonstrations of love, shared history, material or emotional assistance, and other signs of enduring solidarity. (Weston, 109)

We see this dynamic operative throughout McNally's play. Buzz tells the audience at the end of the first act, "All in all, there was a lot of love in Gregory and Bobby's house that first night of the first holiday weekend of the summer" (62). Not warmth, friendship, camaraderie, but love. Yet the family unit also expands during the course of the play. By the end, Ramon, who begins as a date John brings along, ends up being chosen by Gregory to replace him as a dancer. James Jeckyll has been accepted into the family as friend and as Buzz's lover. Even John Jeckyll, however isolated, is still there, invited back time and again. His loneliness and sense of being unloved is greatly a product of his own imagination.

The family supports the illness and aging of its members. Bobby is blind; Buzz and James have AIDS; Gregory is depressed over the waning of his abilities as a dancer. Within the family unit all this is acknowledged, supported.

The most vivid visual image in the play is the sight of six gay men dancing the "Dance of the Little Swans" from *Swan Lake.* The dance takes teamwork and precision: the dancers must move as one. In one sense, the image is hilarious camp—six large men in tutus, ballet slippers, and white, feathered headdresses executing that dainty choreography, but McNally makes the image one of love and community in the face of mortality and AIDS. First James, the most ill of the group, collapses and has to return to bed. Then, as the five continue, one by one they step out of the dance and tell the audience how they are going to die. The dance becomes an absurd, defiant protest against mortality, but it is also an image of family. The dancing is an extension of the group singing that begins the first two acts and ends the third, men's voices blending in nostalgic songs like Stephen Foster's "Beautiful Dreamer." Unity and harmony. Music as the sound of community.

In the play's final tableau, all the characters are skinny-dipping in the moonlight. The nudity is not erotically charged, as Ramon's is earlier in the play. It is nakedness, vulnerability, childlike innocence. The moment has been compared to Thomas Eakins' celebrated painting, *The Swimming Hole,* an idyllic picture of naked men and boys unabashed in presenting themselves for the viewer's gaze.

Love! Valour! Compassion! dramatizes and celebrates a community of gay men in which we see a variety of forms of gay male intimacy: long-time lovers, former lovers who have become close friends, rivals who become collaborators, colleagues who have become friends. Singing together, dancing together, these men comprise an ensemble based on an intimacy idealized by some heterosexual men but only possible when the fear of homosexuality is removed.

IV.

I don't appreciate you flapping your dick in everyone's face, okay?

The once-staid *New Yorker* recently devoted a column to audience reactions to Randy Becker's (the actor playing Ramon) penis.[5] Robert Brustein disdainfully noted:

The major innovation of this play is that virtually everybody in it—and not just the muscled Latino youth (Randy Becker) whom everybody lusts after—eventually gets to take his clothes off. I haven't seen so many pecs and peckers on stage since Oh! Calcutta. *If that's your cup of tea, or piece of cheesecake [beefcake's the word, Mr. Brustein, but, ooh! people might think you're gay if you use it], then you might find some value in* Love! Valour! Compassion! *(Brustein, 31–32).*

Nudity is an important aspect of McNally's play. Ramon's naked body is the object of the characters'—and the audience's—gaze. After a speech addressed to the audience, the beautiful young Bobby does take off his robe and display his naked body at the beginning of the second act. Buzz spends an entire scene wearing only an apron, and all the characters strip for the finale. What is the function of nudity in a gay play? I wrote in *Acting Gay* how in certain plays about gay characters written by straight playwrights (*Six Degrees of Separation, M. Butterfly*) the nude male body comes to figure the threat of the homosexual body, though actually the homosexual body is no different from the heterosexual body.[6] Yet there is a sense in which the willful display of the penis marks one as gay (even if that display is by a straight actor playing a gay character, which only adds to the complexity of the representation of sexuality).

Much of the discussion of the issue of gays in the military was devoted to the trauma for straight soldiers of being looked at in the showers by gay men. Somehow this, above all, would damage military morale. The straight male body, particularly the penis, is to be kept covered. When uncovered, it is not to be looked at. In his book *Running Scared: Masculinity and the Representation of the Male Body*, Peter Lehman notes:

In a patriarchal culture, when the penis is hidden, it is centered. To show, write, or talk about the penis creates the potential to demystify it and thus decenter it. Indeed, the awe surrounding the penis in a patriarchal culture depends on either keeping it hidden from sight (as we see, for example, the classical cinema does) or carefully regulating its representation (as the [straight] pornography film does). (Lehman, 28)

The shameless display of the penis is one of the more radical gestures of McNally's play. Certainly the sight of unclad handsome young actors offers pleasure to the gay men in the audience, and part of the pleasure is the awareness of the discomfort of the heterosexual men to this display. It is, after all, the reaction to the sight of the penis that separates gay men from straight. Love of, fascination with, fetishizing of the penis is the cornerstone of homosexuality. Straight men are not supposed to be interested in other men's cocks, except, perhaps, in seeing how someone else's measures up to one's own. The display of the body, particularly the penis, does underscore the fact that the gay male body is no different from the straight male body, though it is read differently, as straight men see their own bodies differently when they are the object of the gay gaze. For gay men, there is no shame in showing or in looking, and it is conceivable that being looked at empowers more than looking.

In Kevin Elyot's *My Night with Reg*, in many ways the British counterpart of *Love! Valour! Compassion!*, all five older characters become smitten with a good-looking working-class lad from the north who is repainting the host's conservatory. As the play progresses, the young man becomes the moral center of the play as well as the object of the characters' gaze. In the interlude before the final scene, the young man performs a graceful, choreographed striptease. He spends much of the final scene nude. The striptease is not necessary to the action of the play, but it is a sign of its gayness, its open celebration of the pleasure of looking at a male body, particularly the forbidden penis. One *New Yorker* drama critic recently referred to the current wave of penises on the stage as "phallomania."[7] She does not mention that this has been a particular characteristic of gay drama since its beginnings in the early sixties. How else can one capture the importance of looking and being looked at to the gay male experience? While in many gay plays, nudity is only a commercial ploy, in *Love! Valour! Compassion!*, Ramon's nude body and uncovered penis are the catalysts for many of the tensions in the play.

V.

Arthur: Every time I look at Buzz, even when he's driving me crazy, or now James, I have to think, I have to say to myself, "Sooner or later, that man, that human being is not going to be standing there washing the dishes or tying his shoelace."

Perry: None of us is. Are. Is. Are? (121)

In *Angels in America,* AIDS was the unmistakable sign of gayness. Like many closeted gay men, Roy Cohn was outed by AIDS. Prior's bravery and unselfishness in the face of AIDS is one of the signs of his sainthood, perhaps one of the reasons the angels choose him as their prophet of stasis. At the end, Prior has lived with AIDS for five years. Typical of nineties gay plays, the issue in Kushner's and McNally's plays is how one lives with AIDS, not the dying of it. AIDS narratives created by and for heterosexuals (for example, the movie *Philadelphia*) allow the homophobic audience a touch of virtue by allowing them to feel good about the Person with AIDS but always with the knowledge that the death scene would both give them a good cry and rid them of the problem. The disease from which the victim dies is, in the homophobe's mind, not only AIDS but the homosexuality that causes AIDS. In gay society and gay drama, AIDS is an omnipresent reality, but our narratives no longer let the audience believe gayness is a disease nor that gay men are so easily eliminated. People die of AIDS, but they die of a lot of other things as well. We can no longer allow the homophobic audience the victory of our suffering and death.

Love! Valour! Compassion! presents a complex, realistic picture of living with AIDS. Both the comical Buzz and the sweet Englishman, James Jeckyll, have full-blown AIDS, but what we see is the development of a romance between them. We discover that James goes back to London and commits suicide: "I wasn't brave. I took pills. I went back home to Battersea and took pills" (137). But James' recounting of his death is placed in the context of each character's sharing of how he is going to die. Bobby's sister dies in an accident on a ride at a carnival in Jaipur, India. Death is inevitable. McNally does not denigrate the horror of AIDS, but he does want to underscore that gay men not only die; they also live and live happily.

Arthur feels survivor guilt; Gregory plans AIDS benefits. Everyone is aware of and copes with the reality of AIDS, of how many men have been lost and how callously AIDS has been treated by so many straight people. Yet there is no sense of surrender. James claims that his favorite phrase is Hamlet's "We defy augury." Even James's suicide can be seen as a refusal to submit passively to AIDS. James takes control of his own death.

VI.

"They hate us."

In his previous works, *Lips Together, Teeth Apart* and *A Perfect Ganesh*, McNally has dramatized more vividly than any other playwright the outer display and inner workings of homophobia, which is, after all, what gay men most have in common. As many writers have pointed out, lesbians and gay men are the only minority who do not share their minority status with their parents—who are, in fact, usually educated by their parents to believe that what they are is wrong and must be changed or at least denied. McNally has shown us a mother who is haunted by her lack of acceptance of her son and a sister who still cannot deal with her dead brother's homosexuality.

Much of previous gay drama has shown us gay men who hate their own homosexuality, who react in various ways to their internalized homophobia. Even Louis and Joe in *Angels in America* are to some extent dysfunctional homosexuals, if not the sort of basket case we find in Larry Kramer's *The Destiny of Me*. Gayness is not a problem for any of the men in *Love! Valour! Compassion!* Finding what they want and need is.

In Act II, Bobby, Gregory's blind lover, talks to the audience about why he believes in God: "Other people are as imperfect and frightened as we are. We love, but not unconditionally. Only God is unconditional love and we don't even have to love Him back" (87). Yet there is a lot of unconditional love sought and received in the play. McNally commented in an interview:

I've learned as I get older, without unconditional love we never reach our potential. I've had it in my life personally in the past couple of years, and I'm like, "Wake up and smell the coffee. You are so lucky, celebrate this and go, man. The sky's the limit. Why are you holding yourself back?" And this play is just the beginning. (Rosen, 22–3)

McNally prides himself on "the enormous amount of affection and tenderness between men" the play offers (Zinman, 15). It is this sense of love and community that separates *Love! Valour! Compassion!* from other gay plays. One can quibble about the cast being basically white or about the lack of any women, straight or gay, in this world. But this is the only one of McNally's last four plays that does not focus on the strongest, most fascinating women characters in contemporary drama.

Throughout our history, gay men have developed strong positive bonds that are often in sharp contrast with the bitchy, bickering stereotype of much homophobic drama and film. Nor are we the isolated figures of film and television—the queen without a life or society. That is the myth straights use to keep young gay men in the closet. There is a world elsewhere. One of the greatest and most unique virtues of *Love! Valour! Compassion!* is its depiction and celebration of the links of love, loyalty, and patronage that are forged in gay society.

Notes

I have been aided enormously by conversations with my valued students, particularly Gregory J. Tomso, and, as always, with my partner, Walter Melion. Thanks, too, to the friends who comprise my gay community, particularly Bob West, Clifford Hindley, Eric Misenheimer, and Wayland Wong.

1. Now most serious drama is produced Off-Broadway where theaters are smaller and, thus, labor costs are lower. Most of McNally's plays have moved from the Manhattan Theater Club to successful runs in Off-Broadway theaters (*Frankie and Johnny in the Clair de Lune, The Lisbon Traviata,* and *Lips Together, Teeth Apart.*)
2. See my *Acting Gay: Male Homosexuality in Modern Drama,* rev.ed. (New York: Columbia, 1994), 174–181.
3. *A Place at the Table* is an eloquent argument for gay rights but also an attack on the gay left. Bawer argues for assimiliation into mainstream society. *The Advocate* is the national gay news magazine. *Out* is the leading glossy gay magazine.
4. *My Night with Reg* is also set on three different social events at the house of one of its characters. It is a funny yet dark picture of British gay life in the 1990s, yet in a characteristically British fashion it focuses on what makes relationships problematic, if not impossible, for these gay men, rather than celebrating friendship and community as McNally's play does.
5. "Naked Truths," *The New Yorker* (February 13, 1995), 32–3.
6. See my *Acting Gay,* pp.18–27.
7. In a review of openly gay director Sean Mathias's production of gay playwright Jean Cocteau's *Les Parents Terribles,* ridiculously retitled on Broadway, *Indiscretions,* Franklin writes this gem in *The New Yorker* (May 15, 1995):

   For the record, this season's phallomania continues unabated; when [actor Jude] Law gets out of the tub at Madeleine's he takes so long to dry himself off that you could run home, get your binoculars, and be back in your seat before he's finished. (101)

One could add that David Dillon's Off-Broadway success, *Party,* ends with everyone in the buff. The London stage is also filled with nude males this season. D.M.W. Grier's saga of gays in the U.S. military, *Burning Blue,* has a shower scene. Andrew Alty's *Something About Us* contains considerable nudity.

Works Cited

Bersani, Leo. *Homos.* Cambridge, Mass.: Harvard University Press, 1995.

Brustein, Robert. "Aspects of Love and Compassion." *The New Republic,* 3 April 1995: 30–31.

Clum, John M. *Acting Gay: Male Homosexuality in Modern Drama,* rev. ed. New York: Columbia University Press, 1994.

Doty, Alexander. *Making Things Perfectly Queer: Interpreting Mass Culture.* Minneapolis: University of Minnesota Press, 1993.

Elyot, Kevin. *My Night with Reg.* London: Nick Hern Books, 1994.

Kushner, Tony. *Angels in America, Part One: Millennium Approaches.* New York: Theatre Communications Group, 1993.

———. *Angels in America, Part Two: Perestroika.* New York: Theatre Communications Group, 1994.

Lehman, Peter. *Running Scared: Masculinity and the Representation of the Male Body.* Philadelphia: Temple University Press, 1993.

McNally, Terrence. *Lips Together, Teeth Apart.* New York: New American Library, 1992.

———. *Love! Valour! Compassion!* and *A Perfect Ganesh: Two Plays.* New York: Plume, 1995.

"Naked Truths." *The New Yorker,* 13 February 1995, 32–33.

Rosen, Carol. "Terrence McNally: The *TheaterWeek* Interview." *TheaterWeek,* 27 February 1995, 12–24.

Sedgwick, Eve Kosofsky. *Tendencies.* Durham, N.C.: Duke University Press, 1993.

Weston, Kath. *Families We Choose: Lesbians, Gays, Kinship.* New York: Columbia University Press, 1991.

Zinman, Toby Silverman. "The Muses of Terrence McNally." *American Theatre,* March 1995, 12–17.

Chapter Eight
You Got to Have Friends: Gay Reception of *Love! Valour! Compassion!*

Steven Drukman

> *I do believe there is a divinity in all of us, but we run into problems.*
>
> —*Terrence McNally*[1]

> *I think the problem begins right here, the way we relate to one another as gay men.*
>
> —*Ramon in* Love! Valour! Compassion!

"Sex! Velour! Compulsion!" trumpets the unlikely headline of Jeremy Gerard's review in *Variety*, which includes the mind-boggling assertion that McNally's latest play is prurient and sex obsessed to a fault. Gerard writes:

Imagine that a scene in my new play features a beautiful woman, nude and spread-eagled, at center stage. A friendly group of men in various states of undress gather around her, stroke her breasts, and examine various orifices. 'Will you marry me?' asks one, staring into her vagina. Does anyone honestly believe that critics reviewing such a play wouldn't point out the obvious—that at least to some theatergoers, the scenes are prurient and offensive? Yet episodes much like these unfold in Terrence McNally's acclaimed and Broadway-bound new play Love! Valour! Compassion! *The difference, of course, is that the sex object at the center of the action is a gay man among gay men. (40)*

"Episodes much like these" unfold only in Gerard's hysterical imagination. Of course, any reductive straight-to-gay transliteration of theatrical meaning is always preposterous. "Will you marry me?" is rarely uttered by one gay man to another except as a decidedly camp gesture. But even more peculiar, there is no "stroking" or undue "examining" in this play. Nobody stares into, say, any character's anus in *L!V!C!*, obviating any one-for-one semiotic substitution suggested by Gerard, who seems to think that stage signs have some trans-cultural value. While he goes on to say that he "otherwise admired" the play, Gerard complains that nobody "would seriously question the fact that a double standard exists"(40) in the eye-popping sexual display allowed for gay theatre but not for straight theatre. Furthermore, Gerard insists (in that tired old truism) that even many gay men would agree!

I call Gerard's assertion mind-boggling since many of my self-identified queer friends (while having also enjoyed the play, for the most part) have left the theatre with a sour taste in their mouths, complaining that *L!V!C!* felt somehow prudish, remote and decidedly *anti*-sex. What is more, these eight gay characters seemed distinctly unknowable to my queer under-40 friends; friends without country homes, friends "of color," friends who could only afford half-price tickets, who usually shunned the Great White Way. While no play pleases everybody, I was flummoxed as to why, on the one hand, so many straight critics found *L!V!C!* so sex-obsessed, while my queer friends found it so sex-abnegating and, therefore, open to charges of internalized homophobia. Reception of McNally's play has, indeed, been all over the spectrum. I would like to show how *L!V!C!*'s celebration of gay male friendship—a decidedly "gay-positive" message—is sometimes not being heard by both queer and straight audiences.

In an article titled "How Are Things in *Tosca*, Norma?"[2] I applied a mode of gay male spectatorship to McNally's *The Lisbon Traviata* (1989), compared it to examples of the play's mainstream critical reception, and demonstrated how different meanings can be construed by different audiences. Coining the term "gay gaze," I followed a "taxonomy of looking" (at mimetic representation) first drawn by Laura Mulvey in "Visual Pleasure and Narrative Cinema." To summarize Mulvey's 1975 essay, the male spectator identifies with a particular character (Mulvey called this drive "ego-identification") through which his gaze is refracted, often directed at an object of erotic interest (Mulvey called this drive "scopophilia"). Mulvey posited that much of mainstream cinema's narrative moved along this way, with camera shots fetishizing and ego-identifying to provide pleasure for the male gaze.

While the stage gaze is directed very differently than in the cinema, many theatre theorists have borrowed from Mulvey's essay to interpret the workings of reception in the theatre. In my analysis of *Lisbon Traviata*, I concluded that, rather than being (as *The New York Times* called it) a "play (that) embraces domestic banality, as homosexuals repeat clichés from fiction about heterosexual couples" (Gussow, C22), McNally was writing a cautionary tale—a tale in which the gay male spectator is more readily interpellated—in the age of sexual minefields, the age of (what was then called) the "gay plague," the age of AIDS. I surmised that the play's protagonist, Stephen, was in flight from reality, retreating into the ethereal world of nineteenth-century opera to escape the very real and earth-bound world of twentieth-century exchangeable fluids. While the acronym AIDS is mentioned only once in the play, I posited that the gay male spectator received a quasi-Brechtian message in *The Lisbon Traviata* about the perils of sexual engagement in this precarious new world.

I would like to apply this type of analysis to McNally's recent *Love! Valour! Compassion!* to show how McNally's concerns have remained very similar despite different critical responses to this new widely-acclaimed play. I believe that invoking the gay gaze is useful in a close reading of the text, particularly in McNally's approach to "the visible" in *L!V!C!* By concentrating on both visuality as well as this chapter's epigraph regarding "the divinity in all of us," I hope to unpack more thoroughly *L!V!C!'s* approach to gay male sex and friendship—and especially how contemporary gay men negotiate these themes in the age of AIDS—aware that most critical reception has, again, elided these themes by filtering them through a straight/mainstream receptive lens. Finally, I will examine the repeated ways that *L!V!C!* has been received in the mainstream press—especially the disproportionate amount of discussion about male nudity—to round out my analysis of this seminal gay play.

While McNally's *The Lisbon Traviata* is, in many ways, a play about late-eighties AIDS terror, *Love! Valour! Compassion!* expresses a mid-nineties admixture of sadness, remembered rage and resignation. Indeed, while the wages of denial are no less perilous in the last decade of the twentieth century, McNally's more recent play clearly shows a gay male community that has been "in the plague" for almost fifteen years. *Lisbon's* escapist Stephen is not on holiday with *L!V!C!*'s cast of characters, and there is no traditional protagonist in this newer play (although one might argue that the characters embody composites of the absent gay male characters of *Lips Together, Teeth Apart*). Numerous comparisons have been drawn between McNally's play and Mart Crowley's 1968 *The Boys in the Band* in that both plays offer a snapshot of gay men of the moment: Crowley's play is a slice of gay male, pre-AIDS nirvana, McNally's in the midst of AIDS-aftershock and its concomitant blend of anger and torpor.

In encapsulating McNally's encoded gay address in both *Lisbon* and *L!V!C!*, one could do worse than say that the narrative function held by opera (for Mendy) in the former has become musical theatre (for Buzz) in the latter. In fact, Nathan Lane originated both of these roles and has now become closely associated with McNally's plays, especially the characters of Mendy and Buzz. (Incidentally, McNally amplifies my reading of *L!V!C!* in dedicating the play to "Nathan Lane: Great Heart, Great Soul, Great Actor, Best Friend.") But while Mendy's extreme opera fandom functioned as a realm of escapism and denial in *Lisbon* (especially, as I argued, from the terrors of AIDS), Buzz, the aficionado of musical theatre, has evolved considerably. McNally still uses musical-theatre arcana as a wink-and-nod to his gay audience, but Buzz—despite myriad camp quips as well as Lane's comedic acumen—is a far more serious character. He has clearly not retreated from a world of sex and human attachment as McNally marks him as HIV-positive. While he insists that nobody mention AIDS during their time together, he is active in the political fight against the disease. Most important, though, is his last speech about musical theatre, which functions as a grace note to amplify the conclusion of McNally's play:

Once, just once I want to see a West Side Story *where Tony really gets it, where they all die [. . .] A* Kiss Me Kate *where she's got a big cold sore on her mouth [. . .] and they all go down waiting, waiting for what? Waiting for nothing, waiting for death, like everyone I know and care about is, including me. (131)*

While Buzz's call for this type of theatre may sound like *Godot* with chorus girls, it points to just what McNally provides in *L!V!C!*. No tidy happy endings allowed in the age of AIDS (the play's curtain line is an indeterminate and elliptical "Anyway"), McNally's message to his gay audience is sadder, richer, and less proscriptive than it was in *Lisbon*.

The gay gaze is not sutured (in as schematic a fashion) to one character in *L!V!C!* as it is in *Lisbon* but fragmented at various times through various characters. In fact, while Perry acts as the narrator of events (both seen and unseen by the audience) and is therefore the "all-seeing" character for much of the play, direct audience address and asides are taken up by almost the entire ensemble throughout, fracturing narrated perspective accordingly. After the first line, when Gregory directly introduces the audience into his country house, the narrative is guided by the rest of the ensemble in turn (often with explicit audience acknowledgment: for example, "tell them about the sled," [9] "for those of you who know and don't care, I'm really sorry" [16]). This conceit defines the narrative logic of *L!V!C!*: 1) every character is "all-seeing" in this play, and so 2) every character has access to "what happened" in the play and *sees* (or, rather, has already seen) the story unfold. The audience, while gazing at the play's events sequentially and having the plot parceled out to them, remain (literally and figuratively) in the dark.

The play opens with a stolen sexual encounter, a late-night tryst in the kitchen between the two youngest characters, Bobby and Ramon. (I should add here that, for my younger queer friends in the audience, Bobby and Ramon seemed to represent the characters closest to their lives. While beyond the purview of this essay, the position of Ramon as the only non-white character—and the attendant representations of exotic otherness imbricated with his status as sex object—is an aspect worth noting). We will learn that Bobby is Gregory's long-term lover and Ramon is John's most recent conquest. Ramon, more than any other character, is primarily an object of scopophilic interest, for the audience members as well as for all the characters in Gregory's house. Ramon spends most of the second act naked, lying on a raft, and all the characters remark at one time or another about his body and his beauty. Every character, that is, excepting blind Bobby who, even after his kitchen interlude with Ramon, asks Arthur (who has discovered him):

Bobby: Is he attractive?
Arthur: I'm not supposed to notice things like that. I'm in a relationship.
Bobby: So am I. Is he?
Arthur: I think the word is hot, Bobby. Okay? (18)

Later, Arthur admits to having been unfaithful to Perry and advises Bobby not to tell Gregory about this encounter. He tells his blind friend: "He's not that hot, Bobby. No one is" (19).

While McNally constructs a "spectrum of visuality" (with Ramon at the end of the scale of what Laura Mulvey has called "to-be-looked-at-ness"), he also suggests through his characterology a "spectrum of visibility." That is, on one end of this spectrum is Bobby Brahms, the beloved character who is blind and, literally, "sees" nothing but somehow senses all. John, on the other end, tells the audience "I see things I shouldn't" (21), engaged in snooping through Gregory's diary ("words that other eyes were never meant to see"), spying, etc. Collapsed into this spectrum are the two poles of "likability" of these characters, with Bobby representing the most positive valence of love, valor, and compassion and John representing the most negative. References abound to Bobby's "remarkably loving nature" (13), compared to John's "fundamentally hateful one" (14). Bobby is described many times as an "angel" and, even, "too good for this world" (34). Perry deems John "the Prince of Darkness" (68), "John the Foul" (65), and, even, "Adolf Hitler" (35) and "Satan" (33).

But if John cannot connect with people and sees things he should not, what is it that Bobby cannot see but *should*? Bobby, in his love affair with Gregory (an aging dancer), has never seen Gregory dance, nor does he see the scars that (as the audience is repeatedly told) are now mapped all over Gregory's body. In fact, it is John who reflects on the fact that "Gregory's work is the deepest expression of who he is [. . .] and Bobby's never seen it" (23). In a telling exchange between John and Buzz, John muses aloud:

John: I'm puzzled. What kind of statement about his work do you think
*   a choreographer is making by living with a blind person?*
Buzz: I don't know and I don't care. It's not a statement. It's a relation-
*   ship. Remember them? (22–23)*

More to the point, what sort of statement is McNally making here about vision and visuality, especially on the heels of Bobby and Ramon's secret encounter in the kitchen? Of course, Bobby cannot "see" Ramon—the sexually hot and, not insignificantly, young *dancer*—any better than he can see Gregory. Bobby does not "see" and so requires instruction about desirability from Arthur. Still, Bobby's desire bears its own visual trace (semen on his pajamas), just as Arthur exclaims "he's not supposed to notice" the desirability of Ramon.

I would suggest that McNally is configuring within this discourse of vision the idea that seeing *is* desiring, and how dangerous all of this can be. This is evident in the combination of choosing to look away ("**Arthur:** I'm not supposed to notice") with Bobby's blindness and amplified by the satanic John's "seeing things he shouldn't." One might say that McNally lays bare the twin poles of Bobby/Blind/Angel and John/All-Seeing/Satan in Arthur's line (shortly after this encounter): "Desire is a terrible thing" [20]. In *L!V!C!*, it is better to *not* see, to choose blindness, and to connect on some other level altogether.

This is echoed in a flashback sequence that comes soon after the incident described above. Perry and Arthur are driving Bobby to the country house, when Arthur asks Bobby to imagine what people look like. Bobby says: "In my mind's eye, I see very clearly the same things you and Perry take for granted. Gregory's heart is beautiful" (31). This seemingly throwaway allusion to *Hamlet* (Bobby does, in fact, say in the previous line "In my mind's eye, I do, Horatio") will become significant later in the play. Still, Bobby confesses he is intrigued by what John looks like as "after all this time, [he] still can't get a picture" (33). While Perry supplies Bobby with different conceptual images (the aforementioned "pure evil," "Satan," and "Adolf Hitler"), he warns: "Beware him, Bobby. People like you are too good for this world, so people like John Jeckyll have to destroy them." Bobby says that "people like that intrigue me." Still, this back-seat parlor game both teases and frightens the young Bobby Brahms, and he calls an abrupt ending: "I don't like this game. It's making me afraid" (32). Already we get clues that the blind angel is tempted by vision and, by extension, sexual desire.

This is carried over into the next encounter between Ramon

and Bobby, when Bobby, the angel, wearing *white* (it is Memorial Day and much is made of Bobby's sartorial choice) is out in the Edenic grounds of the country house. Bobby has sensed Ramon watching him (McNally writes "he has not taken his eyes off BOBBY" [42]) and tries to make his way to Ramon:

Bobby: *Children play at this and call it Blind Man's Bluff. Imagine your whole life being a children's birthday party game! (43).*

To which, the all-seeing John tells the audience:

John: *Painful, erotic and absurd.*
Bobby: *I can feel you. I can hear you. I'm getting warm. I'm getting close. I like this game. I'm very good at it. I'm going to win. You haven't got a chance (43).*

But Bobby does not win; he trips on a rake, falls and injures himself. Like the semen on his pajamas, desire's dangers bear its visual trace: McNally writes that "there will be a gash on his forehead" (43) and Bobby asks, repeatedly and frantically, "What color are my trousers?" and, then, "Are there grass stains on them?" (43). Gregory remarks how unusual it is that Bobby should fall ("**Bobby:** I do it all the time"/**Gregory:** No, you don't. No, he doesn't" [44]), and finds that he cannot even lift his young lover off the ground, underlining both the metaphoric fall and the literal failure of his aging body. Like the previous game played in Perry's BMW, this accident makes clear the dangers of seeing/desiring. The angel falls, tempted by vision, by sex, and so begins his fall from grace.

There is another game-like moment in *L!V!C!* that is relevant here, overheard and unseen (except by the audience) by characters Buzz and Perry hiding in John and Ramon's closet. The all-seeing John and erotic object Ramon are finally together in their room, a combination that is the most potentially volatile in McNally's schema. Despite the straight press's hysteria, this rather tame scene is the longest sequence actually devoted to a sexual encounter. For my purposes, I want to show how it acts as a *mise en abyme* for *L!V!C!*'s ideas about *thwarting* desire, about looking away from sex and the need to look elsewhere for fulfillment in the age of AIDS. Perry and

Buzz are stand-ins here for the audience, hidden in the dark, eager for the upcoming narrative. The audience's gaze is fractured accordingly: watching the erotic scene unfold (John/Ramon) and watching themselves (Perry/Buzz) eavesdrop.

With Ramon tied to a chair, John asks him "Who do you see?" (94), instructing Ramon to give free rein to his visual fantasizing. Perry tells the audience "we knew what they were doing. We didn't have to see" (95). Ramon then turns the "who do you see?" question back to John, and John begins the story of Padraic the Irishman. Just as Ramon is "bound" on the chair, in John's reminiscence Padraic is bound and gagged, while John is also tied by his wrists and hanging from the wall:

> *John: [. . .] he undressed himself and took a chair, very like this one, and sat in it, maybe five feet away from me [. . .] He looked right at me. He didn't move. Not even the slightest undulation of his hips, and then he came and all he'd let out was this one, soft "oh." [. . .] He moved to whisper something in my ear. My heart stopped beating. He was going to tell me he loved me! Instead, he said, "I've doused this place with petrol. I'm lighting a match. You have three minutes to get out alive. Good luck, 007." (97)*

After Buzz escapes unnoticed upon the story's conclusion, Ramon wants to say goodbye to the departing Bobby. He asks John "Do you mind if we don't?" and adds, "I'm not Padraic." (To which John replies "And I'm not Bobby. C'est la vie" [98]). This scene has the twin effect of allowing us to see Ramon, already marked as an object of the gaze, without *seeing* Ramon—that is, McNally talks about desire without invoking it in the spectator or enacting it onstage. Instead (as in *Lisbon Traviata*) the gay gaze is fractured to receive a warning about the perils of sex: fragmented through Buzz and Perry's reactions in the closet as well as temporal and spatial displacement (the Padraic story mirrors the bound-and-gagged Ramon "story" onstage). Furthermore, these characters are "seeing" different objects—John sees Padraic while Ramon sees Bobby—while the audience sees two men *not* having sex.

McNally draws these two men as not suited to one another in a language of desire, pointing up the cultural differences between these two characters. I use the word "suited" advisedly, as the scantily-clad Ramon can't relate to John's story when he describes Padraic wearing a vest. (**"Ramon:** He was wearing a fucking vest?/**John:** I'm sorry, undershirts you call them" [96]). In fact, the erotic component of this scene is constantly undercut by British colloquialisms misunderstood by Ramon as well as jokes (as asides to the audience) by Perry and Buzz. Finally, it is noteworthy that—while Padraic and John "look but don't touch"—John's story is marked by danger in the image of the inferno and "three minutes to get out alive."

Of course, Perry gets out of the closet alive but not undiscovered by John. Furious, John asks twice, "What did you hear?" (99) and then spits in Perry's face. He then delivers his invective: "I hope you get what my brother has. I hope you die from it" (99). Perry tells the audience he can feel "hate running down my face. So much for the unsafe exchange of body fluids." In keeping with the HIV-positive Buzz's rules, neither John nor Perry mention the word "AIDS" in this exchange of words and fluids. While Buzz sets the rule in order to forget about AIDS while on holiday, McNally sets the narrative conceit for quite the opposite effect. As in *Lisbon Traviata* (where AIDS is mentioned only once), the disease informs all of the above scenes: in the house on fire, in the hate-drenching saliva, and in McNally's encodings of the dangers of vision/desire. These are all pitted against the un"see"able qualities of love, valor, and compassion.

While sex is kept to a minimum in this play, there is another scene where McNally shows fluids exchanged. Bobby swims out to the raft, and Ramon is out there naked, seen by the audience, of course, but unseen by Bobby. Ramon replays the game of blind man's bluff but says that "this time I would let him find me" (71). Ramon prays to "Our Holy Blessed Mother [that he] wouldn't get a hard-on" (71) but to no avail: desire is fighting divinity, making itself visible again. His prayers unanswered, he feels about to explode. Just then, McNally enacts a "double wounding," staging two simultaneous events on different parts of the stage (with both Bobby and Gregory—lovers in different places—exclaiming "Ow!" at the same time[71–72]): Bobby gets a splinter on the raft and Gregory, playing tennis, "falls heavily to the ground" (72). This moment of unbridled sexuality—Bobby groping in the darkness for the erect Ramon—wounds Gregory as much as it does Bobby. Gregory falls,

his aging body deteriorating. Ramon, however, "takes Bobby's fin-
ger, puts it in his mouth, sucks out the splinter and spits it out" (72).
This exchange is not one of HIV transmission but is no less "sexual"
because of it: Ramon has infected Bobby with the taint of desire.

But Bobby's fall is not complete yet. On the heels of his confession to Gregory, Bobby addresses the audience and asks us if we
believe in God. He speaks about the imperfection of humans but
seems to still be inhabiting the liminal space between heaven and
earth. He consoles the audience, "don't worry, I'm not going to fall
off this time!" (87) and tells us that "other people are as imperfect
and as frightened as we are" (87). (Who is this "we"? Gods? Angels?
Other humans?) He seems to have a pipeline to the omniscient deity ("He doesn't have any reservations about me" [87]) but tells us,
finally, that he is human ("It's very unconditional. Besides, he's God.
I'm not" [87]). This is immediately followed by Ramon and Arthur
on the raft, with Arthur ("Desire is a terrible thing") exclaiming:

Arthur: Sun like this makes you want to never move again. I feel nailed
*   to this raft. Crucified on it.*
Ramon: Sun like this makes me horny.
Arthur: Well.
Ramon: I bet I can hold my breath underwater longer than you.
Arthur: I bet you can, too [. . .]
Ramon: Come on! You know you want to! Don't be an old fart! Who
*   knows? We get down there together, who knows what might hap-*
*   pen? (87–88).*

After Bobby's metaphysical aside, this metaphorical exchange seems
more loaded than meets the eye.

The third act finds John "still reading what other eyes were never
meant to see," while his twin brother, the HIV-positive James, has
fallen in love with Buzz. While some critics have complained that
James and Buzz are too easily paired off,[3] the inclusion of James
complicates the binaries of John/Ramon (all-seeing/object of gaze)
and John/Bobby (Satan/angel) in a provocative way. James's presence as John's twin—and, of course, their shared last name of
Jeckyll—suggests that the other side of John lurks within every one
of us, even the most unlovable. While James shares Bobby's bounti-

ful goodness, his being marked as HIV-positive may suggest how far Bobby might fall if he yields to temptation.

On his deathbed, James the Good hears John the Bad's lament:

John: [. . .] You had mum and dad's unconditional love and now you have the world's. How can I not envy that. I wish I could say it was because you're so much better looking than me [. . .] He presses his head against my hand now and cries and cries and cries as I try to tell him every wrong I have done him but he just shakes his head and bathes my hand with his tears and lips [. . .] Finally we stopped. We looked at each other in the silence. We could look at each other at last. (125)

John has found the un-seeable essences of love, valor, and compassion in his self ("We could look at each other at last"), having been cleansed by James's tears, completing the journey from the hyper-visual plane ("I wish I could say it was because you're so much better looking") to a deeper one.

In this final act, there is a moment that is reminiscent of *The Lisbon Traviata*. Gregory—incensed by Bobby's lust for the sexual object Ramon—grabs Ramon's arm, stuffs it into his kitchen sink, and threatens to shred his hand in the garbage disposal. However, unlike the melodramatic gestures of *Lisbon*'s Stephen—where he slices photographs and eventually stabs his disloyal lover—Gregory releases Ramon and turns the momentary melodrama into a gesture of generosity. The strains of age have taken their toll on Gregory's body, and he asks Ramon to premiere his new work of choreography in New York:

Ramon: Where are you going to be?
Gregory: Out front. Watching you.
Ramon: What about . . . (He motions toward Bobby.) (128)

The power of youth, the corporeal and to-be-looked-at-ness are too much for Gregory, and he, too, will be "out front, watching." In this sort of gay-Oedipal reconfiguration, McNally is acknowledging desire's power to steer gay relationships in the age of AIDS. The scene continues:

Gregory: We always said I would stop when it's time.
Bobby: I hate that word. Time.
Gregory: It's time, Bobby.
Perry: You should have seen this man ten years ago, even five. No one
*   could touch him. He's always been some sort of a god to me.*
Gregory: I just wanted to stay like this, my eyes closed, and feel you next
*   to me, our hands touching. Two blind mice now. (129)*

Perry's line to the audience suggests that Gregory has experienced a
sort of fall as well, from an untouchable god to an aging choreographer. Although desire later bears its visual traces (John, reading
Gregory's diary tells us that Bobby and Gregory make love later,
"kiss[ing]so hard [they] each had hickies afterward" [129–130]), we
find out by play's end that Bobby's fall is complete: he leaves Gregory for an unseen character, Luke.

Before the play's conclusion, each character addresses the audience squarely and, in turn, relates the story of his death. It is a theatrically rich and logical moment, as death has permeated the play
from the beginning. It is no tidy ending, either, as we learn that
James ends up coming short in the valor department (he goes home
to Battersea to swallow pills) and John—despite his absolution—
dies alone and unmourned. McNally has Ramon tell us: "I don't die.
I'm fucking immortal. I live forever" (138). Although this is undercut by an actual story of mortal death (Ramon, it turns out, dies in
a plane crash), McNally seems to suggest in this line the eternal and
immortal nature of sex, desire, and the seduction of youth. Bobby is
the only character who "doesn't know" how he dies, but Gregory
informs him: "You won't be with me [. . .] It was my age./**Bobby:**
No./**Gregory:** It was my age./**Bobby:** Yes" (138).

The play ends, significantly, in a power failure's blackout, an
environment where one can't be distracted by sexual display, and
one where an angel like Bobby is in his element. All the men go
skinny-dipping, but Bobby stays behind to clean up (Cleanliness is
next to godliness, of course). After the recounting of their deaths,
this scene takes place outside of real time, as a coda of sorts:

*(James enters. He is wearing a robe. He watches **Bobby**.)*
Bobby: Who's there. Somebody's there.

James: It's me. Forgive me for staring. You looked very handsome in the
moonlight. Very handsome and very graceful [emphasis mine]. I'm
going to remember you like that. It's James.
Bobby: *I know. Are you supposed to be down here?*
James: No. And neither are you. (141)

It is interesting that Bobby could never get a picture of John but
knows right away that his *visual* twin, James, is in his midst. It is also
significant that James tells Bobby that he will remember him like
that when James (as we all know) is about to die. (In other words, if
this scene were more literal, wouldn't Bobby be remembering James?)
But it is a remembrance for the John/James Everyman—the character to whom we ultimately suture our gaze as he represents all of
us—and so it is a bittersweet remembrance of *L!V!C!* that McNally
intends for us. We all can fall from grace and all forget love, valor
and compassion. There are no easy answers when desire captures
our eyes and complicates the picture. But Bobby should be with the
angels, as he is the character who never "dies" for the audience (as
James replies when asked if he is supposed to be *down* here: "No.
And neither are you.") But as John, the other half, declares in a
curtain line with a decided lack of closure: "Anyway" (142).

Anyway, the critics had their own ideas about McNally's play.
The infamous John Simon (of *New York* magazine) titled his review:
"Saucy! Schmaltzy! Slow Moving!" with the sub-head announcing
"*Love! Valour! Compassion!* has the problem of all the jokes being
sexual. Is there no other kind of humor?" (79). Not a critic slavishly
tied to textual evidence, Simon cites many jokes from the play, with
very few actually addressing (directly or obliquely) the subject of
sex. Still, Simon was not alone in decrying the ostensible prepon-
derance of sexual subject matter and display of the male body in
McNally's play. Vincent Canby of *The New York Times* stated that,
while he admired the play, "there will also be those who say its total
effect depends on male nudity" (5). Nancy Franklin of *The New
Yorker* (3) wrote that Bobby and Ramon were there for "mainly youth
and beauty" (66). On the other coast, *The Los Angeles Times*'s Laurie
Winer said that the play's "voice is an interesting counterpoint to
the characters' frank expressions of desire for the nude male form,
which several of the characters display without being asked" (23).

The Financial Times gasps that "frontal nudity is rampant in this play" (Fricker, 20) and *The Christian Science Monitor* moans that "the play's up front and at times crass attitude toward nudity and sexuality will put off many theatergoers" (Scheck, 14).

Apparently, when confronted with the naked male body—alive, present and on display—many critics simply went into phallic over-drive. David Richards, in a lovely and insightful review in *The New York Times* (he notes that in the world of this play "all bids for grace are similarly clumsy and brave" (C15) still can't resist calling Ramon "a snake let loose in Eden" [C13]. Naturally, critics gay and straight alike are going to have some fun with punnery about McNally's pe-nile colony, but it is unfortunate when spectatorial anxiety about the naked male form occludes *L!V!C!*'s theme of friendship's triumph in the age of AIDS. In the most amusing instance of seeing penises everywhere (and, therefore, unbridled homosexual erotics), Robert Brustein complained that McNally (in an act of authorial masturba-tion, I suppose) was now "stroking the gay audience" (31). I quote at length from Brustein's review in *The New Republic*:

Instead of being an advance in gay playwrighting, Love! Valour! Com-passion! *looks more like a regression to* Boys in the Band *[. . .] the play has no real subject other than sexual relationships—who is sleeping with whom and how the who and the whom can be rearranged [. . .] McNally has a sharp edgy wit and he certainly knows how to feed bananas to hungry spectators. I probably wouldn't have found this evening so unap-petizing were it not for the author's compulsion to shovel serious issues into the comic casing, in the manner of a butcher stuffing feed down the neck of a goose in order to enlarge its liver [. . .] The major innovation of this play is that virtually everybody in it—and not just the muscled Latino youth (Randy Becker) whom everybody lusts after—eventually gets to take his clothes off. I haven't seen so many pecs and peckers on stage since* Oh! Calcutta *(31).*

Of course, Brustein also complains about the gay address in *L!V!C!* (e.g., "such favorites as Judy Garland and Glenda Jackson" [31]). And yet, he misses the message of John's line, abandoned on stage, addressing his audience: "**John:** 'And I am all alone.' That's from a song. What song. Anyway" (130). McNally's gay audience knows that the song is the over-the-top anthem "(You got to have) Friends," a canonical camp classic made popular by gay icon Bette Midler—the "*Divine* Miss M."—in the 70s. But one can only expect so much from straight critics. Even the elliptical "anyway" becomes, in John Simon's overwrought language, a "*sweaty* factotum," having to provide even the curtain line." (79, emphasis mine).

Perhaps the "real" curtain line of *L!V!C!* should be James's Act III quip to his lover, Buzz: "We defy augury" (114). James claims to have no idea what it means, but the line is uttered by Hamlet to Horatio (always listed in the dramatis personae as "*friend* to **Hamlet**), before his deadly duel with Laertes. Theatre scholars will recall that Hamlet has just said to his friend: "There's a divinity that shapes our ends, rough-hew them how we will." Then, later in the scene: "**Hamlet:** We defy augury; there's a special providence in the fall of a sparrow [. . .] Since no man has aught of what he leaves, what is't to leave betimes?"

Angels and sparrows fall; mortals die untimely deaths, and no man knows how he will be remembered by posterity. James's absolution of John is for naught, as John dies alone and unloved. And while sexual desirability is both immortal and mortal (like Ramon) and hovers in the ethereal realm of mortal angels (like Bobby), AIDS has brought to the fore the need for love, valor, and compassion. Neither sex crazed nor anti-sex, McNally celebrates the familial bonds formed by gay men as friends. For as many gay men in the audience heard from McNally, and, no doubt, already know, "you got to have friends." It is Ramon—the plot-hinge and bimbo with a brain—who tells the audience and, especially, the gay audience, what McNally means when he says "I think the problem begins right here, the way we relate to one another as gay men." In this way, we defy augury indeed, and McNally has penned a hit, a palpable hit.

Notes

1.   Personal interview, October 1993.
2.   See my essay "Gay-Gazing at *The Lisbon Traviata* , or: How Are Things in *Tosca, Norma?*" in *Theatre Topics*, volume 5, no. 1. (March 1995): 23–34.
3.   e.g., Michael Feingold's "Gender Is the Night" in *The Village Voice*, November 9, 1994.
4.   I should also mention an amusing item that illustrates fractured reception in *The New Yorker's* "Talk of the Town" section. In a tidbit titled "Naked Truths" (February 13, 1995), various audience members—listed alongside their sexual orienta-

tion and New York neighborhood (e.g., "Gay Man, Chelsea", "Straight Woman, Upper East Side")—checked in with their opinions on the size of Ramon's penis. Apparently, Becker's stature had become the "talk of the town," indeed.

Works Cited

Brustein, Robert. "Aspects of Love and Compassion" in *The New Republic*, 3 April 1995: 30–31.

Canby, Vincent. "McNally, True, But Vaguely Neo-Chekhovian" in *The New York Times*, 6 November1994, Sunday ed.: 5, 32.

Drukman, Steven. "Gay-Gazing at *The Lisbon Traviata*, or: How Are Things in *Tosca, Norma*?" in *Theatre Topics*, volume 5, no. 1 (March 1995): 23–34.

Franklin, Nancy. "McNally Men, Wasserstein Women" in *The New Yorker*, 14 November 1994.

Fricker, Karen. "Drama on Off-Broadway" in *The Financial Times*, 26/27 November 1994: 20.

Gerard, Jeremy. "Sex! Velour! Compulsion!" in *Variety*, 21 November 1994: 40.

Gussow, Mel. "A New, Non-violent Ending for 'Lisbon Traviata'" in *The New York Times*, 1 November 1989: C22.

McNally, Terrence. *Two Plays: Love! Valour! Compassion! and A Perfect Ganesh*. New York: Plume, 1995.

Mulvey, Laura. "Visual Pleasure and Narrative Cinema" in *Screen*, volume 16, no. 3. (1975): 6–18.

Richards, David. "In the Hearts and Minds of Men Who Love Men" in *The New York Times*, 2 November 1994: C13–C15.

Scheck, Frank. "'Uncommon Women' Ages Poorly, McNally's Latest Has Its Strengths" in *The Christian Science Monitor*, 15 November 1994: 14.

Simon, John. "Saucy! Schmaltzy! Slow Moving!" in *New York*, 14 November 1994: 79–80.

Winer, Laurie. "In the End, 'Love!' Prayers Are Answered" in *The Los Angeles Times*, 15 November 1994: 23.

Chapter Nine
A Perfect Ganesh:
McNally's Carnival in India

Benilde Montgomery

When, in Terrence McNally's *Lips Together, Teeth Apart* (1992), Sally Truman looks over the Atlantic and laments that "the truth is just too formless to grasp" (22), she might be speaking for McNally himself. Impelled by the shifts, epistemological and otherwise, occasioned by the abiding presence of AIDS at the center of post-modern culture, McNally creates in this play and in its successor, *A Perfect Ganesh* (1993), a context within which he hopes that death, particularly untimely death, can recover a significance and meaning far more publicly and historically grounded than the balloons he released during the improvised ritual which ends *Andre's Mother* (1990). Consequently, in *Lips Together,* McNally surrounds death with the traditional symbolism of pastoral and pastoral elegy, utilizing, thereby, the tradition that shaped a similar search for, for example, Theocritus, Virgil, Milton, and Whitman. Unlike theirs, however, McNally's contemporary quest fails. Pitting the traditional symbols of western pastoral (water, stars, music, ivy, etc.) against the magnitude of AIDS and the isolation of contemporary life, he finds not only that the symbols are now hollow but also that the cohesive gay community whose lives and music had once kept the symbols alive is so besieged that the symbols atrophy and dissolve. At play's end, the saving water of tradition is contaminated, the stars crash randomly into the sea, the music is ignored or trivialized, and the heroic ivy is poisoned. Unlike Milton's Lycidas, McNally's drowned young man is a suicide who does not become the "genius of the shore" but washes up with the tide, a parody of Milton's shepherd and ultimately the victim of scavenging thieves. Still hopeless, the suburban protagonists sit in a twilight reverie, as the efficient "zap" of a machine steadily wipes out the offending bugs.

The tone and outcome of *A Perfect Ganesh,* however, are remarkably different. The Western elegy having failed him, McNally turns to the East and to Hindu legend. Again using traditional material, he seeks in it a form where, as Sally says, things will not fall apart. In *Perfect Ganesh,* although Katharine, an American suburbanite like Sally, protests to any Hindu who will hear that she is "sick of your mythology. It's as false as ours. My son was not reborn," her anger is premature. Soon afterward, her dead son does indeed appear to blow her a farewell kiss (97). In *Lips Together, Teeth Apart,* reconciliation eluded the suburban visitors because they refused to participate in the Independence Day celebration to which their gay neighbors invite them. In *A Perfect Ganesh,* however, the outsiders accept their parts in a play about the god Ganesha's story, Ganesha himself telling them that "in India we participate in theater . We don't sit back, arms folded and say 'Show me'" (87). The result is that, as in traditional festive comedy, the visitors return from the unformed world of India, reconciled, renewed and reborn (89). McNally's Ganesha proudly reminds us that India is "fully independent" (27) and that "the main thing to know" about it is that it is "the largest democracy in the world" (32). For McNally, the Hindu myths succeed where the Western myths fail because they are still vitally alive among the general population and just not among a dying and invisible elite. Consequently, they are irresistible and have power enough to transfigure the commonplace, even death, in a way that Western mythology, it seems, no longer can.

As in *Lips Together,* the protagonists in *A Perfect Ganesh* are strangers in a strange land. Armed with guidebooks, they come to India from "the *gotterdammerung* of American civilization" (6) with analogous and troubled pasts. Similar but quite different, both women suffer from the mutilating deaths of their sons: Margaret Civil, aloof and starchy, learns to mourn the loss of her four-year-old Gabriel, accidentally run over by a black woman many years before; and Katharine Brynne, "vivid, forthright, an enthusiast," learns to mourn the loss of Walter, deliberately murdered three years ago by a black, gay-bashing mob. Needing healing from guilt and loss, they come on a deliberate spiritual quest. Appropriately, they are overwhelmed by the unexpected, including specific incidents of the Ganesha narratives which echo their own story: like them, the goddess Pavarti dotes on her young son, Ganesha, and suffers bitterly when his head, too, is violently crushed. Disturbed by these correspondences, revolted by the sight of lepers, and sickened when the corpse of a baby boy smacks against their skiff on the Ganges, they return to Connecticut able to "allow, accept, be" (19).

Moreover, as McNally abandons Western mythology so does he also forego his own traditional realistic style, adopting a new theatrical, presentational one: Ganesha himself functions as narrator and actor, the dead manifest themselves to the living, and, with the exception of the two women, all other characters are played by only two actors. This stylistic shift has caused difficulty for some critics. One dismisses Ganesha as "less a tutelary deity than as a practical supernumerary" (Brustein, 32); another blames the "economics of Broadway" for the doubling (Torrens, 22); a third complains that things "needn't be this confused" (Richards, H17). As he appears in Hindu mythology and as McNally's play re-creates him, Ganesha suggests, however, that things *are* this confused. Certainly, in the story of this Indian god and the effects of his power on two American visitors, reality cannot be reduced to the disjunctive categories of psychological realism and the representational theater. The actor playing Ganesha never in fact "doubles" roles at all. He remains consistently Ganesha, never becoming absorbed into any of the other characters for whom he speaks, thereby allowing the audience to understand these numerous others (a tourist, Mr. and Mrs. Watanabe, a carpet sweeper, a train porter, a playful child, etc.) not only as separate characters but as manifestations of the one god, Ganesha. This kind of role playing is consistent with Ganesha's description of himself: I am "everywhere . . . in your mind and in the thoughts you think, in your heart whether full or broken . . . I am in what you eat and what you evacuate . . . I am in your kiss. I am in your cancer" (3).

Properly seen, Ganesha is an instance of what historians of religion call the *coincidentia oppositorum*, "the most basic definition of divinity," "one of the most primitive ways of expressing the paradox of divine reality," a divine "unity which signifies not the chaos that existed before any forms were created but the undifferentiated *being* in which all forms are merged" (Eliade, 419–420). In appearance, he is god and elephant; in outlook he is child and adult; in manner he is masculine and feminine. Speaking of infants, he says, "[Is there] a sweeter smell than their soiled diapers? *There's* a place to bury one's face and know bliss!" (4). He later speaks of a "concept . . . so important to me . . . that opposites can live together happily" (69). As the embodiment of such fullness, Ganesha's "doubling" is a necessary means through which McNally symbolizes a metaphysical reality: Ganesha is both author and participant, weak and powerful, Japanese and American, laborer and manager, leper and god. Similarly, since such a vision of unity in diversity underlies the protagonists' quest, a similar "doubling" occurs in the character of "Man" who, like the god, is all sons, all husbands, all tourists, all doctors, all lepers. To support this, Katharine frequently notes the resemblance between these apparently discrete characters and her dead son, Walter. To hear the echo between the divine and the human, between the god's story and our own, and to apprehend beneath the diversity of appearance what Rose Zimbardo calls "the great cosmic *concordia* that lies beyond the boundaries of human sight" (2) are the unsuspected fruits of the women's journey and the object lessons of the play.

In addition to this, McNally's specific depiction of Ganesha resembles Bakhtin's definition of "clown." This suggests that in *Perfect Ganesh*, McNally is quite consciously going beyond the limits of traditional "festive" comedy to something more like "carnival." Like Bakhtin's clown, Ganesha stands in "a peculiar midzone" from which he can mediate the ideal and the real, life and art (8). As such, he presides over the threshold that separates audience and play, actor and character, and over the border that separates the "official" world of appearance, which enslaves the two woman at the play's start, and the "second world" they eventually discover, an alternative and different world in which their conventional values are annulled. McNally also introduces many other components of carnival: a "multiplicity of styles," a "disclosing of the unvarnished truth," a "heteroglossia" that excludes the "authoritarian world," "ritual spectacles," "comic verbal compositions," "genres of billingsgate." As in carnival, these liberate the women from their familiar "established order" (10) and assure the renewal they crave. At play's end, unlike their counterparts in *Lips Together,* their isolated Western egos have been dissolved; under Ganesha's tutelage and under the carnival spirit over which he presides, they no longer "exclude themselves from the wholeness of the world" (Bakhtin, 12) .

McNally also suggests the world of carnival by setting the central events of the play during the Hindu feast of "Hali" [sic.] (4; 83), a Saturnalia-like, lunar feast which celebrates spring, or as Marriot puts it, "world destruction and world renewal" (212). One of its unique features is "shouting obscenities accompanied by appropriate gestures directed particularly at women and passersby" (Walker, 354). To further assure us that India is not the familiar holiday world of "festive" comedy but the more primitive world of "carnival," McNally's characters continually note that their trip is an "adventure" (14) for "my soul" (18), not the "annual, same old two weeks in the Caribbean with the Civils" (23), not "the same old Shinola" (36). Ganesha tells us that "vacations can end abruptly. . . . Trips have a way of going on. Mrs. Civil's and Mrs. Brynne's visit to India was of the second variety" (108).

In addition, the "heteroglossia" of carnival that is one aspect of the destruction of the characters' familiar world is evident in Ganesha's first speech (in English with interpolations in French, Spanish, German, and Italian) as well as in a number of conversations about language, apparently in Hindi but perfectly comprehensible to us. McNally compounds this by also including many diverse styles of English: the gracefully accented English of Ganesha; the Shakespearean English of both Katharine and Harry (39, 41) and Ganesha, who quotes Puck (22); the lurid English of a movie soundtrack (13); the flat English prose of travel guides and self-help books; the street-talk of the gay-bashers (24; 97); McNally's signature lyrics from musical comedy (67); translated lines from a Hindi playbook (87–90); and, significantly, not the lyrics of opera but the simple English lyrics of folksongs (110). This diversity of styles, moreover, points out not only the variety of language but also its inadequacy. Like the Prologue to *Henry V,* Ganesha says at the start that "we have to imagine" what we are going to see (4). Consequently, the play, set on a bare stage "which has been painted blinding white" (3), demands an engagement that realism frequently thwarts. It points always beyond the illusory phenomena that prevent Katharine and Margaret from apprehending the truth symbolized by Ganesha. Like Sally Truman, Katharine remarks, "How hard it is to really describe anything" (37), and even her own repetition of the Prologue's actual "O for a muse of fire," which itself expresses this inadequacy, becomes an obstacle between her and Margaret and must eventually give way to "Offamof" (85), made-up syllables which parody ordinary language but which come finally to express the otherwise inexpressible.

A further aspect of carnival here is what Bakhtin's translator calls "billingsgate" (5), abusive, violent invective, a specific characteristic of Holi. Among the examples of billingsgate are mockeries of the deity, of Ganesha himself.

Katharine, for example, imagines that his name "sounds like a Jewish food" (33), and Walter rejects his chiding by calling him an "old man" (23). He is most mocked, however, when he "doubles." Mr. Biswas tells him (as a maid) to "shut up" and threatens to have him fired (61); Margaret threatens to have him (as a porter) reported for molesting her (79); Katharine calls him (as Mr. Watanabe) "one very outspoken Jap" (46). All these and numerous other abuses suggest, of course, that the speakers do not yet recognize the god beneath his characters' appearances. McNally thereby suggests that most people fail to appreciate the inseparable reality of the human and the divine (or what Ganesha names the "insignificant magnificent" [12]). Rather, like the characters in *Lips Together,* they see human beings simply as discrete phenomena divorced from any metaphysical scheme, their blindness thereby reducing most ordinary human interaction to blasphemy. To the modern Western eyes of the audience, the very presence of the god as woman, slavey, leper, clown, and child is "carnivalesque" and a clear affront to orthodox, pious expectations.

McNally also employs the billingsgate of carnival to indicate his characters' growth in freedom from their familiar and "official" culture. As in the feast of Holi, invective here becomes a form of purification. For example, alive, Walter dared not accuse Katharine, but, in India, he can dismiss her guilt and vilify her homophobia because it effectuated her complicity with the black mob who murdered him ("No, mother! All of them you!" [25]). Although Margaret appears more victimized by political correctness ("keep your voice down"), Katharine's propriety is even more debilitating because it gags her rage, preventing her from cursing her son's murderers. Ganesha, recognizing that "she needed upsetting" (89), first contextualized her own story by forcing her to play her counterpart in his own myth:

she must read the role of the beheading parent, Shiva. Then, assuming the role of a playful child ("My little brown bambino, my nutmeg *Gesu*" [95]), Ganesha teases her into shouting the curses that the social conventions of her Western respectability forbid: "Fag! Queer! Cocksucker! Dead from AIDS queer meat! . . . Faggot! Queer! Nigger!" (97). Katharine, we are told, "begins to break down," but the ensuing freedom allows her, like Shiva, to beg the forgiveness of her mutilated son, who, in turn, forgives her. She is at last able to mourn. Ganesha must still remind her, however, that, although she did not know it, all along she had held "a god in her arms."

Billingsgate thereby destroys the false egos the women bring from the modern West. But like the "marketplace speech" of carnival, abusive speech here is also "ambivalent: while humiliating and mortifying, [it] at the same time revive[s] and renew[s]" (Bakhtin, 16). While unmasking the characters, invective discloses to them the clarity of unaccommodated truth. A porter whom they find charming actually wants to show them "a most excellent view of my ass" (29). Another says, "These are Jew Christian old whores with white saggy skin. Their shit is on your tongue from all the ass licking" (33) . Margaret Civil, among whose delusions is her sensitivity to other people, is the frequent and appropriate target for many of these curses. Katharine, for example, finally calls her a "pain in the ass" (38), and Walter sees her as a cold-hearted "bitch" (23). After she sneers at him, an "Aging Hippie" tells her that she has "cruel eyes. They're filled with hate." He tells Katharine, "Your friend needs a good purge in the Ganges. I don't think she's ready for Katmandu yet. There's not enough dope in the Himalayas to mellow that dude out" (21). We are reminded of this curse when towards the end, Ganesha, "the queller of obstacles" (3), completes Margaret's purification by actually splashing her with water from the Ganges. Her defenses crumbling, she humbly asks, "What are we supposed to do? I can't accept all this . My heart and mind would break if I did. And yet I must. I know it" (101) .

In all versions of the Ganesha story, his beheading by Shiva is the "inevitable and necessary" condition for the emergence of his new, divine identity and of his real power (Courtright, 89). While the analogy between the mythic beheading of Ganesha and the literally crushed skulls of Gabriel and Walter situates their deaths within a cosmic scheme, that is, makes them something other than simple phenomena, the violent unmasking of their mothers deepens the analogy even further, giving the Ganesha myth a more universal resonance. While the women imagine their trip as a failure because they did not do what they set out to do, it, nonetheless, transforms them. Imperceptibly, the "natural" yields to the "spiritual," with McNally's suggesting, as do most spiritual writers, that the seeking and the finding are in fact inseparable and constitute a dialectical continuum. Katharine's and Margaret's desire alone is enough for Ganesha, "the Lord of Beginnings, the guarantor of success" (Courtright, 6).

McNally indicates this success in several ways, one of which is, as in carnival, the development of a "new, purely human" (Bakhtin, 10) relationship between the women. This relationship grows as together they come to understand the unvarnished truth about death: death, like poverty, they discover, is not an emotion, but a fact (32). When Margaret protests that Harry and his lover will soon die, Ganesha's simple answer is, "Why not?" (53). When Katharine refuses to read Shiva's role with, "Why me, Mr. Tandu?", Ganesha answers, "Again why not you, Mrs. Brynne?" (89). Ganesha, however, respecting the differences between the two, treats each woman quite differently. In some ways he is gentler with Mrs. Civil, whom he identifies as "the nice one" (60), possibly because she "travels light" (8) and has already forgiven her son's killer. Nonetheless, when, at first aloof and suspicious, she discovers in her Bombay hotel that she has cancer, she allows Ganesha, as Mrs. Watanabe, to touch her breast. Accepting her gift of a Japanese kimono, she literally puts on the unfamiliar and accepts that her own way of being in the world will be irrevocably different. Although Margaret can never speak of Gabriel's death, after Ganesha splashes her with Ganges water and takes away the binoculars which have kept India at a safe distance, she allows Katharine also to touch her breast. To understand Margaret's cancer as a fact of human experience, moreover, and not as a discrete, private tragedy, McNally interrupts them with the cry of a leper in the streets. Transferring her question from Margaret to him, Katharine asks, "Why are you diseased and hideous? What can I do to change that?" (104). His response, like Margaret's implicit response and Walter's earlier spoken one, is "Love me." Still unable to touch the leper as she thinks she ought, she, nonetheless, can finally and fully embrace her friend, Margaret.

Because the extremities of Katharine's enthusiasms create greater obstacles to her enlightenment, Ganesha deals with her more violently. She does not "travel light," and so Ganesha impoverishes her by not only unmasking her but also by depriving her of those material obstacles which blind her to the truths he represents. Significantly, he replaces these lost material objects with figurines of himself. In the first act, Katharine's suitcases fly open (5), she leaves a flight bag behind (11), and her cassette player, with its signature Western music ("Frank Sinatra and Mozart and Cole Porter" [28]), is stolen. By the second act, she has discovered the god Ganesha and begins a typically obsessive search for his perfect image. As Ganesha takes away Margaret's binoculars, however, so he begins to take away Katharine's statuettes as well (102), until, with Ganesha telling her that all his images are perfect, Katharine herself chooses to give her favorite Ganesh to Margaret (106). Katharine's final impoverishment is her husband's death, reported not as personal tragedy but as cosmic, objective fact." . . . some 8,345 miles away at 11:20 P.M. their time, George Brynne . . . Caucasian male, aged 62, lost control of his car . . . and slammed into a 300-year-old oak tree" (85). Katharine's success is clear when she can echo Ganesha's cosmic view and accept this death "better than expected" (109).

Common to all the illusions that both Margaret and Katharine bring with them from the familiar "ordinary" West to the other, "carnival" East is, of course, the illusion of the omnipotence of their own wills. Margaret, for example, moves through the airport with Machiavellian assurance, abusing a clerk who suggests she has "vanished without a trace into the vast netherworld" of the computer system (9). Having recently "nurtured her inner child" and equipped with audio-tapes of her "10 Personal Power Goals," Katharine's first mantra becomes "I choose to be happy . . . I choose to be healthy . . . I choose to be good" (133). No doubt, seeing India "from a comfortable seat, somewhat at a distance" (10) preserves the supremacy of their egos, and as long as Katharine listens to her tapes and Margaret observes the Indian mob from her balcony, their wills remain unchallenged. Consistent with this disengagement is their mistaken notion that the means of their salvation lies within the powers of their own wills. Katharine especially hangs onto romantic stories, perhaps learned in her Catholic childhood, that kissing lepers, as St. Francis did, will appease her guilt. When her two dramatic attempts at this fail, Ganesha reminds us that while Katharine "worried about her soul," the leper at whom she threw her coins fed his body and "had the finest meal of his entire, miserable life" (105).

And, ultimately, it is the very bodilyness of India that unmasks the impotence of the human will and reveals to Margaret and Katharine that their assumptions about its absolute power are based on little more than a privileged ideal. Guided by the potbellied god with the elephant's head who loves nothing more than the smell of soiled diapers, they are confronted everywhere by "the given"—the concrete and inescapable parameters which define the limits of every human life. Unlike the suburbanites in *Lips Together*, however, who remain in helpless isolation before these same limitations, Katharine and Margaret are finally able to appropriate "the given" to themselves. Having seen their own lives universalized in myth, a myth whose symbols remain vivid and active in "the largest democracy in the world," they know now from their own experience that in Ganesha's cosmic view, "things will simply not fall apart." In accepting what they have experienced as "inevitable and right," in understanding that in Ganesha's view "nothing is right, nothing is wrong" (101), and in attempting to harmonize their circumscribed and tragic vision with his comic and universal one, they achieve, almost in spite of themselves, the liberation they seek. That they have achieved this awareness is clear when, standing with them before the Taj Mahal, Ganesha asks, "What does one say before such beauty? If one is wise, very, very little." Margaret, uncivil and abrupt, silences an American tourist who reads from a guidebook, and Katharine, for the first time, adds, "I don't think I can talk" (107).

Hinduists tell us that in the evening of public festivals in honor of Ganesha, his clay image, like that of Adonis in Western myth, is brought to the water's edge and ritually submerged (Courtright, 202–247). Dissolved into the sea, Ganesha becomes part of the wholeness of the world. Returned to Connecticut, the women receive a postcard asking if in India they, too, did not "die just a little?" (109). Indeed, as we finally see them, Ganesha reminds us that their renewal is incomplete: Margaret, wed to an adulterous husband, still remains silent about Gabriel, and Katharine, recently widowed, still needs to be coaxed into affection. Although the differences between them remain, they have, nonetheless, "become the very best of friends" (39). And when Ganesha finally appears and stands between their beds to sing them both to sleep, we are reminded of that other pair of opposites over whose reconciliation Ganesha continues to preside: Shiva and Pavarti. Standing between them, Ganesha mediates the cosmic forces that make life itself possible.

Works Cited

Bakhtin, Mikhail. *Rabelais and His World*. Trans. Helene Iswolsky. Bloomington, Ind.: University of Indiana Press, 1984.

Brustein, Robert. "Travel Packages," *New Republic*, 23 & 30 August 1993: 32.

Courtright, Paul B. *Ganesa—Lord of Obstacles, Lord of Beginnings*. New York: Oxford University Press, 1985.

Eliade, Mircea. *Patterns in Comparative Religions*. New York: Sheed and Ward, 1958.

Marriot, McKim. "The Feast of Love," *Krishna: Myths, Rites and Attitudes*, ed. Milton Singer. Honolulu: University of Hawaii Press, 1966.

McNally, Terrence. *Lips Together, Teeth Apart*. Garden City, New York: Fireside Theater, 1992.

———. *A Perfect Ganesh*. Garden City, New York: Fireside Theater, 1993.

Richards, David. "Sunday View," *New York Times,* 11 July 1993: H17.

Torrens, James S. "A Perfect Ganesh," *America,* 14 August 1993: 22.

Walker, Benjamin. *The Hindu World*. New York: Praeger, 1968.

Zimbardo, Rose. *A Mirror to Nature*. Lexington: The University Press of Kentucky, 1986.

Chapter Ten
Terrence McNally on *Master Class*

from interviews with Toby Silverman Zinman

TMcN: Maria Callas was a great musician, a great expressive artist. The most interesting thing I can say about me in relation to Maria Callas is that when I was growing up in Texas, I fell in love with the sound of her voice—I had no idea what she looked like. Most people now who are obsessed with Maria Callas are obsessed with the myth of a woman who was rejected by Onassis, who was glamorous—she was none of that for me. She was a voice coming over the radio. I'm so glad I have what I think is an honest relationship with her—she was a young singer, no one in America had heard of her. There's a scene in *Lisbon Traviata* we cut where Stephen talks about how it annoyed him that everybody was now on the Callas bandwagon— we cut it because it didn't mean anything to the audience—it was a minute-long speech of Stephen's about hearing her as just a voice. By the time I heard Judy Garland she was a myth—I never just heard this voice and said, "Oh, I love this singer; who is it?" So I approach Callas totally as a sound. You didn't have to have seen her—everything that was her genius is in the records. She was a dramatic-looking woman, quite beautiful, I think, but I've seen more spontaneous in-the-moment actors—I think Gwyneth Jones is a better actress; I think Elizabeth Schwartzkopf is and Leonie Rysanek—I don't think Callas ever did a spontaneous thing in her life on stage. She could create the illusion of that, but Callas prob- ably moved less than 99% of the other singers—she stood and she drew you to her; she held herself when she sang—she struck won- derfully artful poses, but most of the time she was still.

Callas in recital was the same person as Callas in costume play- ing Tosca. The drama, the beauty, the genius of Callas are on the albums. With a lot of singers, if you didn't hear them live, you didn't hear them, but Callas recorded very well. I saw Callas maybe twenty-five or thirty times, which, for an American is an extraordinary amount. There are many Callas authorities, like John Ardoin—I don't think he ever heard her sing live. At the end, the last recitals, I kind of wish I hadn't heard them—it was painful—she was like a broken bird, a dying swan.

TZ: Why did you choose *Macbeth* for the end of *Master Class?* Is the content significant?

TMcN: I wanted a contrast to the Bellini in the beginning, and it's an exciting aria—you get to speak in it when you read the letter. Callas was not a famous Lady Macbeth—she only performed it four times. It was a short career—six seasons at La Scala—the brevity of her golden years, compared to say Tibaldi's forty-five years at the Met or the fortieth anniversary of Resnik's debut—it's quite a difference.

   There are other singers I admire, but I think it's because Callas was so important to me as an adolescent—it's an enormous intensity but always within the boundaries of art. You take as much raw passion as you can and still express it in the classical form. That's the kind of art that appeals to me—lots of sopranos scream and sob and shriek, but with Callas it's in the actual singing—the genius is in the coloring of the voice. That's what a great writer does too—it's the same instrument from play to play but you find new colors. So that *Master Class* will never remind anyone, ideally, of *Love! Valour! Compassion!.* Of course, I can't reinvent my personality for each play, but I can find new colors to express my feelings.

TZ: Does an audience need to know about opera to respond to *Master Class?*

TMcN: We had a good response to a reading we did in Montana from people who don't know anything about opera. One question during the discussion afterwards was: "was Maria Callas a real person or a character?" The next day, I was with Zoe [Caldwell] on the little main street and someone stopped us and said they'd really enjoyed the play and said to Zoe, "are you a professional actress? you're very good." This must have been the kind of audiences Sarah Bernhardt was playing to when she booked *Camille* into the mining camps.

I think this play is about playwrighting—about the need for art, about what we do with our enormous feelings, how we can keep some sanity—I don't think this play is about Maria Callas and opera.

And *Master Class* is an homage to teaching. I dedicated *Frankie and Johnny* to my high school English teacher, Maurine McElroy—I wanted to dedicate something to her she would hear of in Texas, that was out in hardback, not just script form. I've been asked to speak at the LBJ library (two weeks from tonight), and she's in Austin, about to retire after heading the freshman English program at Texas University for the past twenty years, and after the speech, you go upstairs and have a small dinner with Mrs. Johnson. She's going to be my date. I think my mother is a little put out that I didn't ask *her* to come to Corpus for this evening, but I said, you've been such a Republican all these years, how could I ask you?

TZ: How did you decide to write a play about Maria Callas?

TMcN: Zoe Caldwell—there is no actress like her, that's why I want to work with her again. [Zoe Caldwell played Katharine Brynne in *A Perfect Ganesh* which opened on June 4, 1993, at the Manhattan Theatre Club]. I heard Zoe give a speech from *Ganesh* as part of a benefit program, and I went home that night started writing about Maria Callas with Zoe Caldwell in mind.

TZ: What kind of style do you want here—is this operatic acting? One of those let-er-rip performances? Every speech she has is an aria.

TMcN: What makes it different is she's really talking to the audience. Three people come out of the audience to actually sing. Zoe delivers 110%—she's not a minimalist—I've never believed that less is more.

TZ: More is more.

TMcN: More is better. [This part of our conversation took place over dessert, while he was eating a giant plate of profiteroles and making massive resolutions to go back on his diet.] I respond to her sense of theatre—it's larger than life.

TZ: Opening a new play of yours with Zoe Caldwell in Philadelphia—well, we're all atwitter. Are you thinking of Philadelphia as a try-out town, as it used to be? Or is this a long dress rehearsal? I heard it was booked for Broadway.

TMcN: It's booked for Broadway if the reviews are good here. It would have to be a whole new physical production. But I think this kind of cooperation between regional theatre and New York is an inevitable thing with the decline of the road. Philadelphia Theatre Company did a wonderful production of *Lips Together* [1993] and I love the space, and I think it's very apt for this play.

I'm very excited about doing it here. The mortality rate of plays in New York is as high as it is precisely because so many plays are done cold now. When I first came to New York, every show went to Philly, Boston, Washington—you thought nothing of seeing a head-line, "*Fiddler on the Roof* postpones opening a month," "*West Side Story* will be staying out another six weeks." You didn't say, "oh, that's in trouble," you figured, they're working on it. *Love! Valour! Compassion!* has changed so little from the first preview to the one you saw on Broadway. "Try-out" always sounds as if you know there's something wrong with it, but plays take their final step in front of an audience—the audience is the final character added to a play.

Chapter Eleven
Interview with Zoe Caldwell

Toby Silverman Zinman

Editor's Note: The following interview with Zoe Caldwell took place on December 9, 1994, on the telephone; she was at her country house, and I was in her husband's (Robert Whitehead) office on Broadway.

She is full of apologies since she forgot our appointment in New York—having just finished directing Vita and Virginia *(which had opened to fine reviews the week before), and trying to get ready for Christmas since they were leaving for the Bahamas the next week. Upon her return, she would start work on the role of Maria Callas in* Master Class, *for which she would win in 1996 the Tony for Best Performance by a Leading Actress in a Play, as well as The [Philadelphia] Barrymore Award for Outstanding Performance by a Leading Actress in a Play.*

Zoe Caldwell, one of the great actors of the English-speaking stage, began acting professionally as a child in Australia. Once she came to England as a young woman, she played Bianca to Paul Robeson's Othello and Cordelia to Charles Laughton's Lear. Besides being one of the great Shakespearean actors, she won her first Tony for her performance in Tennessee Williams' Slapstick Tragedy *in 1966 and her second Tony for* The Prime of Miss Jean Brodie. *Her Medea won her a third Tony, and since then she has worked in everything from one-woman shows (Lillian) to Mary in* Long Day's Journey Into Night *with Jason Robards, to classics filmed for Canadian and British television. She continues to direct as well, including an* Othello *with Christopher Plummer and James Earl Jones and the recent* Vita and Virginia, *with Vanessa Redgrave and Eileen Atkins.*

Her voice—that famous, thrilling voice—is, even on the telephone, deep and rich with a complicated accent that is Shakespearean over native Australia; her conversation is full of italics and full-throated laughter, and the sense of instant intimacy—immediately on the phone she said to me: "I'm 61. How old are you?" Her speech is punctuated by reflective pauses—moments of absolute silence (no "ums" or murmurs)—she takes questions seriously and thoughtfully and her responses spiral toward their conclusion. This is not a linear mind.

TZ: This will be your second McNally play in a short space of time [*A Perfect Ganesh* in 1993]. What appeals to you about his work?

ZC: I think theatre should make you laugh—and so did the Greeks. And weep—and so did the Greeks. Once upon a time Terrence's plays made you laugh, and as he grows as a playwright and a man, he can make you weep.

Terrence's exploration of something profound began with *Lisbon Traviata,* and that traveled into *Ganesh*—tapping something in us all that troubles us today—guilt, inadequacy, and what we do to cover those feelings. He has enormous skill and something philosophically *true.*

We live in strange times—don't you think so? Books are written that give us solace, or you can rent a video and sit at home, but we truly need theatre because it's a communal thing.

Terrence has never abandoned the theatre as so many playwrights have. He is the way playwrights *used* to be—he writes a play a year [this year two]. His whole absorption is as a true theatre person. When we went looking for theatres for *Master Class,* he was truly amazing. Everyone was saying it's too big, it's too small, it's too long, it's too short, but he would tell stories of what plays he'd seen there, what actors played there.

He writes for actors—which is rare—and he writes with a particular actor's voice in his head. And he is quite determined to *get* that voice for his play.

TZ: Are there similarities between the characters of Katharine in *A Perfect Ganesh* and Maria Callas in *Master Class*—something lavish, excessive about both women, a temperamental extravagance?

ZC: No. Katharine's lavishness is that of a Connecticut housewife. Maria's was that of a tragic artist.

TZ: And how often we mistake the one for the other.

[We both laugh.]

TZ: Are you a Maria Callas fan?

ZC: I am now. I never saw her. Of course everybody spoke about the master classes at Juilliard, but I never went, I suppose I didn't care enough then. I'm so protective of her now—when I hear people who are about to tell some terrible anecdote about her, I don't want to listen.

I spent two wonderful hours with Sheila Nadler, who was one of the terrified singers in her master class.

TZ: Did her experience match that of the play?

ZC: Yes—she *taught.* Her master classes were "good parenting." Maria felt that the singer was [ZC suddenly compresses her vowels into a European accent, with explosive consonants] the "servant of the comPOSer"—that's the way she said it.

TZ: Is this your attitude, as an actor, toward playwrights?

ZC: Many actors don't obey the playwright, but words are the nitty gritty of the play.

Watching the tapes of Callas do *Tosca,* if you were deaf and just watched her, you'd be perfectly satisfied—she could act. [It is interesting to note here that McNally said precisely the opposite; see interview.]

Her life was a true Greek tragedy.

TZ: As something of a legend yourself, what it is to embody someone else who is a legend?

ZC: You are very kind. I like doing that. I've done it before, with Collette, with Lillian Hellman (Lillian was the most painful). As McNally told Leonard Foglia, the director, his Maria is not the historical Maria, this is not a documentary.

But it does require enormous preparation. That is my pleasure. I have to learn to speak Italian fluently; I have to learn three arias (of course I don't have to sing them, but I have to *know* them with great ease)—I have to evoke Maria, not impersonate her.

TZ: Do you think the opera queens will turn out for this and react to you as a reincarnation of Callas?

ZC: I hope not—that could be taken as an act of terrible hubris.

TZ: The young soprano's speech at the end [she tells Callas, ". . . I don't like you. . . . I hate people like you. You want to make the world dangerous for everyone just because it was for you" (61).] Do you think the audience might react to your character that way?

ZC: If I can do the right work in the right way, it will look after itself. I don't mind playing a character the audience doesn't "like"— When I played Medea I wanted consciously to look *not* appealing— I wanted the audience to feel "I don't know if I want to spend two hours with her"—that's the way we react to people who have been deeply hurt. But—with God on our side, we can come to compassion.

There are sophisticated audiences in Philadelphia, and that's a lovely little theatre—we're very lucky.

TZ: In one of your speeches in Act Two, you tell one of the students, "A performance is a struggle. You have to win. The audience is the enemy. We have to bring you to your knees because we're right." Do you feel that way when you act?

ZC: I know that the power must never go into the audience, it must remain in your hands. The audience members singly are okay, but an audience is a composite of all those intelligences, limitations, emotions—and that animal is *tremendously* potent. I wish the audience in our theatre was freer to make itself known—to say, "louder!" if they couldn't hear. You throw your boot at a screen and the actor will go on, but if you throw your boot at a live actor he will react— the *real* communication is that we are alive. I *love* that—so did Maria Callas. Terribly aware of the living performance.

I had a copy of the last radio interview Ralph Richardson did for the BBC—he talks about how he liked actors to be dangerous. That's what audiences want. Maria knew that.

TZ: Since you also direct, do you find it difficult to take direction when you're acting?

ZC: No, they are different creatures. When you're directing you're a parent. When you're acting you're a child, sibling of all the other actors, all trying to get approval and attention from the director.

TZ: You seem to choose to play women of strength—Vita, Virginia, Medea, Lillian, Maria. What is your interest in such women?

ZC: I'm not a particularly strong, powerful woman myself. Perhaps you should ask my husband [Robert Whitehead]. What truly turns me on is when someone has been born with a certain disability and overcomes it. I am thrilled by individuality—[here she quotes from Martha Graham's autobiography, *Blood Memory*] "The main thing, of course, always is the fact that there is only one of you in the world, just one, and if that is not fulfilled then something has been lost. Ambition is not enough; necessity is everything." I love it when people fulfill their individuality. Usually they have humor and they are not afraid of their uniqueness—they take hold of their own destiny, and, boy, did Maria do that.

Chapter Twelve
Callas and the Juilliard Master Classes

John Ardoin

Opera is frequently found at the heart of the theatre of Terrence McNally, either as a means or as a metaphor. But in at least two of his plays, *The Lisbon Traviata* and *Master Class*, opera becomes a dominating force. Casting a long shadow over both these plays is the monolithic figure of the late Maria Callas. She has been a magnetic figure in McNally's life, and in his introduction to my book, *The Callas Legacy*, he has this to say about Callas and the potency of her art:

Like most people, I first heard the voice of Maria Callas on a record. It was an appropriate introduction to a singer whose career was relatively brief and whose actual performances in this country were few.

The year was 1953, the recording was Lucia di Lammermoor, *and I was a high school student in Corpus Christi, Texas, who bussed tables at the Robin Hood Cafeteria in order to buy opera records. I was fifteen, a dreamer, and I thought she was singing just for me. I still do.*

Listening to Callas is not a passive experience. It is a conversation with her and, finally, ourselves. Callas speaks to us when she sings. She tells us her secrets—her pains, her joys—and we tell her ours right back. "I have felt such despair, such happiness," Callas confesses. "So have I, so have I!" we answer. It is ourselves we recognize in Violetta or Norma or Lucia when we listen to Callas sing them.

No one before her "heard" Lucia the way she did. Nor had they been able to articulate Donizetti's music with such deep and specific feeling. Lucia became a recognizable human being. The Fountain Scene was an expression of both tragic foreboding and ecstatic first love. The Mad Scene became the cumulative threnody for that love betrayed when the forebodings become reality.

All at once, it was possible to care about Lucia. She had become a human being. As she did with almost everything she sang, Callas changed our very perception of the role and its possibilities. In so doing, she not only gave us Donizetti's heroine but she also changed the face of opera. After Callas, Lucia, Lucia di Lammermoor, *and the entire bel-canto repertory would never be the same. We are still dealing with and reeling from her revolution. . . .*

But to a fifteen-year old in South Texas, she was necessarily a voice without a face. She was the Queen of La Scala in Milan, I was a busboy at the Robin Hood Cafeteria on South Staples and never, surely, our twain would meet. The records would have to suffice. And so I loved her as a blind man must come to love someone: with all my other senses engaged. Her voice was *her face, and I came to know and love almost every feature of it through her many recordings. It is still the best way to know Callas. And now it is the only way. . . .*

When I named a play of mine, The Lisbon Traviata, *the tape of that performance had not yet surfaced. The title was thus meant to represent the mythic, the unobtainable. Since I completed the play, EMI has released the performance and it is readily available. I wonder if I wrote a play called "The Chicago Trovatore," "The Venice Walkure," or "The Genoa Tristan"—equally legendary performances of which tapes are rumored to exist—would EMI oblige us again? If I thought they would, I would begin all three plays today. . . . (xi–xiv)*

The Callas of *The Lisbon Traviata* is the mythic Callas as perceived by others—Stephen and Mendy, two best friends, both opera fanatics, both ardent record collectors. *Master Class*, however, is Callas on Callas. McNally puts her center stage, takes us into her mind and makes us privy to her needs, her fears, and her dreams.

The play, however, is not solely a tribute to an influential, mesmerizing operatic diva but to the act of performance and to the commitment and communication necessary to make art. It is, in short, an investigation of what it means to be an artist. As McNally has Callas remind us,

A performance is a struggle. You have to win. The audience is the enemy. We have to bring you to your knees because we're right. If I'm worried about what you're thinking about me, I can't win. I beg, I cringe for

your favor instead. . . . You have to make them beg for yours. . . . Art is
domination. It's making people think that for that precise moment in
time there is only one way, one voice. (37)

McNally audited the master classes Callas gave at the Juilliard
School in New York over two decades ago. They remained vivid in
his mind, and, under the spell of the penetrating art of actress Zoe
Caldwell, he found a way at last to give his memories dramatic shape.

Though *Master Class* has several characters in addition to Callas, they are more props than people; the play is, in effect, a one-
woman show. In investigating his theme, McNally attempts to enter
the mind and personality of Callas and create what he imagines her
to have felt and been obsessed with at this point in her life. In short,
he shares Callas's secrets with us as he perceived or wished them
to be.

As for the real Callas, her demons, her needs, and the actual
classes, let the facts show how well McNally honored both the needs
of theater and of his subject:

In 1971, Maria Callas was restless. Her gilded apartment in
Paris seemed more often a cage than not; she had few close friends,
and her days became longer as they became emptier.

She had not sung publicly in six years; her last recording session
had ended inconclusively; the hope for a career in films had fizzled,
and her personal life was in disarray.

The pressing need to work, which had always pushed her forward, demanded an outlet—anything to take her mind off her problems and give her back some of the sense of purpose which had
sustained her during the glory years at La Scala.

She was working diligently on her voice, trying to understand
what had gone wrong and searching for a way to set it right. But this
in itself was not enough to fill her days and her long, insomniac
nights. She had lost the one man she truly loved, Aristotle Onassis;
she lacked nerve and a belief in her ability to conquer, and she was
terrified of appearing again before an audience, of having to recreate
the specter of Maria Callas, a monster figure she neither understood
nor particularly liked.

Then came the offer to undertake a series of master classes at
New York's Juilliard School of Music. It must have seemed like a

heaven-sent resolution to her stalemate, one that served virtually all her needs. It would occupy time and keep her fevered mind busy; it would enable her to try her voice before an audience without carrying the burden of officially performing even so much as an entire aria; it would help build her confidence, and it offered an opportunity to articulate the musical ideas that had cropped up as she attempted to realign her voice. And perhaps by putting Callas on exhibition, Maria could better understand her other and long-dominant self.

So, in the spring of 1971, she came to New York and held auditions to pick the singers that would constitute her class at Juilliard in the fall. Three hundred applied; she chose twenty-five.

For twelve weeks between October 1971 and March 1972, she presided over the stage of the Juilliard Theatre like, as one observer put it, "a Delphic oracle." The parade of young hopefuls performed standard arias for Callas and a paying audience (at $5 a head, it was the best entertainment bargain in New York that season). They sang not just excerpts from Callas' repertory but from a wide range of operatic literature that stretched from that for mezzos and tenors to baritones and basses.

This was the format: In her studio the afternoon before each class, Callas privately sang through all the music that was to be covered that day with pianist Eugene Kohn, the accompanist for the classes. Then promptly at five P.M., she moved to the stage for a two-hour work session.

Callas was usually dressed casually but elegantly in slacks and a blouse, with her long, shining auburn hair left loose and brushed back. Her huge eyes and the sharp profile that looked as if it had come from an ancient coin were extended by a pair of heavy, horn-rimmed glasses.

She frowned at any attempt on the part of the audience to applaud, and the first day she cut short an outburst of homage with a rasping, "None of that. We are here to work."

And work she did—serious, concentrated, dedicated work that placed her, her voice, her personality, and her ideas squarely at the service of the students. Callas may have had ulterior motives in undertaking the classes, but once she did, she was there unstintingly for her students. This was no ego trip.

She helped in a practical, down-to-earth manner. From the outset it was obvious that Callas wished to bring out the best in the talents of those who sang for her rather than try to impose herself on them to produce a string of mini-Callases. She demanded faithfulness to the score and its style, and she carefully explained what this consisted of. She insisted on individual expression, of course, but always within the context of the notes.

Rarely did Callas simply order a student to "Do this. . . ." Rather she said, "Do this because . . . " and gave them reasons based on the score and rooted in tradition. When the mood moved her or she needed to express herself beyond words, she used her voice. There were days when it was little more than a croak, and she was honest about it: "I'm not in voice today," she would say simply, and let it go at that.

But then there were days when the miracle occurred—the miracle one secretly hoped for but never dared to dream would happen, when that unique, portentous, dark sound of hers flashed out with strength and security to brilliantly illuminate a phrase with the power of a searchlight.

In such moments it became clear just how starved we were for that unique sound of hers that had been denied us since her last public appearance in 1965 and how much we hoped it was not too late to experience it again in some semblance of its former glory. But that, alas, was not to be.

On the whole, Callas was disappointed in the singers she worked with at Juilliard, and, of those who took part in the class, only Barbara Hendricks had a career of significance. One can readily understand Callas's disappointment, for too often the students appeared solely wrapped up in themselves and their sounds. They rarely seemed to hear what Callas was offering them and continued to make the same mistakes and sing the same way from class to class. This was the main reason the classes were not repeated a second year.

At the last class, Callas said good-bye with these words, words which are exactly echoed by McNally on the final pages of his script for *Master Class:*[1]

I am not good with words, but there is one thing I would ask of you: that our efforts not be wasted, that you do not forget what little I have given you. Take it and apply it to other scores, so that your phrasing, your diction, your knowledge and your courage will be stronger—especially your courage. Do not think singing is an easy career. It is a lifetime's work; it does not stop here. As future colleagues, you must carry on. Fight bad traditions; remember we are servants to those better than us—the composers. They believed; we must believe.

Of course, by helping the composer we help ourselves. But this takes courage—the courage to say no to easy applause, to fireworks for their own sake. You must know what you want to do in life, you must decide, for we cannot do everything. Everyone seems in a hurry today—too much so, I think. Conductors frequently do not have the time to know what these scores are about. You must show them in a nice way what is necessary to the composer and why. This is what I have always tried to do, and what I have wanted to instill in you who will follow.

Whether I continue singing or not doesn't matter. What matters is that you use whatever you have learned wisely. Think of the expression of the words, of good diction, and your own deep feelings. The only thanks I ask is that you sing properly and honestly. If you do this, I will feel repaid.

Callas's ego, her capacity for hard work, and her myopic vision of her world are conveyed with unerring directness by McNally. *Master Class* never makes a false or superfluous step.

By the time the classes were over and done with, Callas had found the courage to return to the stage. She undertook an extended concert tour the next year with tenor Giuseppe di Stefano that was a search for her lost identity. Callas had always said that she was driven to sing more by the will of others—her mother, her husband, and now a lover—than by her own will. But this time what also drove her back to the stage was her determination to show Onassis that she was not the one who was in need but that she was the one who was needed. The tour, however, proved the opposite. It was not what she or we wanted it to be or hoped it might be; it turned out that her need for us was even greater than ours for her.

Notes

1.   Editor's note: Ardoin is quoting from an early version (April 1994) of the script (ms, 74). It is worth noting that McNally rewrote this final speech, altering it considerably in the final version (see the Plume edition, pp.61–62); this is consis-

tent with his having created a play about a dramatic character, not a documentary of the historical Maria Callas.

Works Cited

McNally, Terrence. Introduction to *The Callas Legacy* by John Ardoin. New York: Charles Scribner's Sons, 1991.

Chapter Thirteen
Master Class and the Paradox of the Diva

Cary M. Mazer

Master Class begins with a double untruth. Maria Callas (or, more accurately, the actress playing Maria Callas) strides on stage, almost certainly to the accompaniment of the audience's applause, looks directly at the audience, and announces, "No applause. We're here to work. You're not in a theatre. This is a classroom" (1).

The first untruth is the statement that we are not in a theatre, since we in fact are in a theatre, both outside of and within the fictional world of the play.[1] In *Master Class*, the stage of the theatre represents the stage of a theatre—the recital hall at the Juilliard School, where Maria Callas gave a series of master classes in 1971 and 1972 before a full house of students and spectators. In the theatre, when *Master Class* is performed, it is, of course, not really 1971 but the present; it is not Juilliard but (for the play's Broadway run) the Golden Theatre; and the audience is comprised of paying theatregoers, not advanced voice students. But the audience is *there*, as an audience, in both the reality of the theatrical event and the fiction of the play. The actor may be (in the original production) Zoe Caldwell and not the "real" Maria Callas, but the response of the audience to Caldwell—applause—is the same response that the 1971 Juilliard audience (the fictional audience that the real audience pretends to be) has for Callas. For Caldwell/Callas to tell us that we are not in a theatre flies in the face of what we know to be true, both in life and in the fiction of the play.

The other untruth is that Maria Callas does not want applause. Maria Callas, we soon see, lives for applause, and thrives on having an audience, alternately revealing and concealing herself from it, pandering for its affection and sympathy and holding it in contempt. Later in the play (60) she will even deny that she had asked the

audience not to applaud. Maria's attitude and her philosophical pro-
nouncements are filled with such contradictions: that we cannot
know what she suffered in Greece during the war and that we have
to know it; that one can only create art if one has suffered and that
one must not bring one's private suffering to one's art; that singers
sing for the sheer joy of it and that singers must never give away
their talent except for sufficient pay, etc., etc. The paradox of the
audience's simultaneous presence and absence, of the fiction's theatricality and non-theatricality, is mirrored by Maria Callas's opinions—at best paradoxical and at worst contradictory and mutually
exclusive—about life, art, performance, and their relationship. And
at the heart of these paradoxes is the real subject of the play, what
one might call "the Paradox of the Diva."

Terrence McNally has dramatized the phenomenology of the
diva before, most notably in what might be considered the ultimate
play about "opera queens," *The Lisbon Traviata*. But there the focus
is not on the diva but on her fans, the homosexual protagonists who
project onto the diva their own identity, desires, and suffering. In
The Lisbon Traviata the opera queen's identification is both with the
singer and with the operatic role she plays: both with Maria Callas,
the self-consuming performer who makes her private suffering transcendently public through her performances, and with Violetta, the
consumptive courtesan in *La Traviata*, who sacrifices her happiness
and her health for love.

McNally is not interested in the phenomenon of the opera queen
in *Master Class* (though in one of the flashback sequences, Maria
ventriloquizes the voice of her lover Aristotle Onassis, who observes
"The fags just want to be you" [26]). Instead he shifts his focus to
the object of the opera queen's emulation, the diva herself. But the
way he views the diva is clearly in line with the paradoxes and contradictions in the way opera queens admire and emulate the diva, a
phenomenon most recently articulated in Wayne Koestenbaum's
autobiographical polemic, *The Queen's Throat: Opera, Homosexuality, and the Mystery of Desire*. The opera queen, Koestenbaum argues, admires both the diva's persona—her arrogance, grandeur, and
self-fashioned hauteur and sublime bitchiness—and the roles that
the diva plays. Indeed, the opera queen's identification with the roles
the diva plays magnifies the opera queen's emulation of the diva, for

the diva, the opera queen believes, identifies with the character even more closely than the opera queen ever can and so becomes the opera queen's emotionally expressive, sacrificial surrogate. As Stephen, one of the two opera queens in *The Lisbon Traviata*, explains, "Opera is about us, our life-and-death passions—we all love, we're all going to die. Maria understood that. That's where the voice came from, the heart, the soul, I'm tempted to say from some even more intimate place" (61). At the end of the play, Stephen, having failed to enact Don Jose to his departing lover's Carmen, throws his head back in a silent scream of heartbreak while Callas's Violetta plays on the stereo, the diva's voice expressing a pain that is simultaneously the singer's, the character's, and the listener's.[2]

The diva, the subject of the opera queen's emulation, is simultaneously present and absent, playing a distilled and self-fashioned version of herself in every role she plays and dissolving herself into the music and the dramatic situation of the character she acts and sings, rendering herself transparent to the character and the composer (and librettist) behind the character. The difference between the actor and the character she is playing is erased in the eyes of the opera queen: the diva is both transcendently herself and transubstantially the character; indeed, that is to a great extent the source of her glory.

But the relation of an actor to the character he or she is playing is, in the theatre as well as in opera, much more complicated and more paradoxical than the opera queen imagines. And this complicated relationship of actor to role—the paradoxical complementarity of the consummately self-effacing actor and the transcendently-herself diva—is the real subject of *Master Class*, a play in which the opera-singer-as-lecturer is not "in character" ("You're not in a theatre. This is a classroom") and yet is never, strictly speaking, "out" of character, in which theatrical performances draw upon the performer's true "self" and yet the "self" is itself always performative.

The salient biographical facts about Maria Callas's life are all made reference to in *Master Class*: her American and Greek upbringing, her training, the patronage of Battista Meneghini, her debut, her radical physical transformation and weight loss, her affair with Onassis, her conflicts with tenors, managers, directors, and rival sopranos, the hirings and firings, and the precipitate decay of her voice.

But the play is less a biography of the artist than it is a play about the nature of artistry, the relation of a particular artist's life to her art. The paradoxes of this relationship are both the play's subject and dictate the play's form, and these paradoxes ultimately lead to a shift in the play's focus that muddies the play's focus and, as we shall see, finally undoes the play's otherwise pristine structure.

The play's action, such as it is, consists of three consecutive coaching sessions in real time: Sophie de Palma, a soprano, who sings Adina's "Ah, non credea mirarti" from Bellini's *La Somnambula;* Anthony Candolino, a tenor, who sings "Ricondita armonia" from Puccini's *Tosca;* and soprano Sharon Graham, who is driven from the stage by Callas's brow-beating but returns to be coached in Lady Macbeth's entrance aria, "Vieni! t'afretta" from Verdi's *Macbeth.* In each of these sessions, Callas is rude, condescending, dismissive, and egocentric. And in all three sessions she is a brilliant teacher. And there emerges from her teaching, however obnoxious, a coherent, if complex, philosophical position about the relationship of the singing actor to the operatic role.

Callas interrupts the first note that Sophie de Palma sings in the Bellini aria: "I want to talk to you about your 'Oh!'" The student answers, "I sang it, didn't I?" Callas explains:

That's just it. You sang it. You didn't feel it. It's not a note we're after here. It's a sob of pain. The pain of loss. Surely you understand loss. If not of another person, then maybe a pet. A puppy. A goldfish. (13)

Mixed with Callas's patronizing examples ("a puppy. A goldfish") is a stereotypical "Stanislavski Method" acting exercise—Lee Strasberg's "emotional memory"—in which the actor substitutes an experience from his or her own life to generate an emotional response equivalent to the emotions of the character that are called for in the dramatic situation of the script. Callas repeatedly rejects "just singing" ("You were *just* singing," she tells the tenor, "which equals nothing" [40]). Instead she calls for acting, in the twentieth-century Stanislavskian tradition: feeling "real" emotions based on the "given circumstances" of the script and embellished or translated in the imagination of the actor (when the tenor complains that "It doesn't say anything about ten A.M. or spring or Tosca's body in the score,"

Callas responds, "It should say it in your imagination. Otherwise you have notes, nothing but notes"[43]).

The emotions that Callas calls for are not "realistic"; they are channeled through the artifice of the operatic medium ("Anyone can walk in their sleep," she tells Sophie, singing a somnambulist's aria; "Very few people can weep in song" [11]). Each successive level of expression in opera is more artificial: speech is more active and demands more actively channeled emotional energy and a more intense revelation of one's own more intense emotions than silence; recitative calls for more energy and emotion than speech ("When you can no longer bear to speak, when the words aren't enough, that's when he [Bellini] asks you to sing" [18]); aria more than recitative; and a cabaletta more than its preceding aria.

"This is not a film studio," she explains, "where anyone can get up there and act. I hate that word. 'Act.' No! Feel. Be. That's what we're doing here" (16). And she later tells Sharon, helping her "make an entrance" for her Lady Macbeth entrance aria, "This is opera, not a voice recital. Anyone can stand there and sing. An artist enters and *is*" (35). What Callas means by "be" and "is" is clearly something more than passive existence or inexpressive emotion and is rather a grand, artificial, projected distillation of one's identity and emotional truth: as she tells Sophie, "This is the theatre, darling. We wear our hearts on our sleeves here" (11). When she tells Sophie "I'm not getting any juice from you, Sophie. I want juice. I want passion. I want you" (16), she clearly means that the "you" that an opera singer needs to "be," the being that breathes and feels and sings on stage, is something grand, extreme, distilled, and directed. Callas doubts whether Sophie has that magnitude of experience or the magnitude of expressiveness: "He's broken her heart. Have you ever had your heart broken?" she asks. When Sophie answers, "Yes," Callas adds, snidely, "You could have fooled me" (11); and Sophie herself concludes, ruefully, "I'm not that sort of singer. . . . I'm not that sort of person either" (16).

What "sort of person" does it take to be an opera singer? Here again there are both paradoxes and contradictions in what Callas teaches. On the one hand, she claims on her first entrance, the diva must practice complete self-effacement: "If you want to have a career, as I did—and I'm not boasting now, I am not one to boast—

you must be willing to subjugate yourself—is that a word?—subjugate yourself to music" (2). But, paradoxically, the singer both erases herself and is completely herself. For subjugation involves sacrifice, and what is being sacrificed is the singer's own self. The diva must be a supreme egotist in order to make the supreme sacrifice of her ego to her audiences. And, she argues, you must be well paid for your pains. "Never give anything away. There's no more where it came from. We give the audience everything and when it's gone, *c'est ca, c'est tout. Basta, finito.* We're the ones who end up empty" (32). She invokes Medea's line to Jason in Cherubini's *Medea*—"I gave everything for you. Everything"—to explain this: "That's what we artists do for people. Where would you be without us? Eh? Think about that. Just think about it while you're counting your millions or leading your boring lives with your boring wives" (32). The sacrifice of the self is too great to be wasted on psychotherapy: "Feelings like Sharon's"—who has run off stage to vomit and has not yet returned—"We use them. We don't give them away on some voodoo witch doctor's couch" (40). Instead, they should be saved for the stage, where they are distilled and delivered, at great personal pain, to the audience.

Callas's relation to her audience—both the audience of her operatic past and the current audience in the classroom/recital hall—is fraught with contradictions. "The audience is the enemy," she says, quoting Medea's line to Jason; "Dominate them. . . . Art is domination. It's making people think for that precise moment in time there is only one way, one voice. Yours. Eh?" (37). At times (including the flashback sequences, in which Callas recalls singing only for Meneghini or only for Onassis), the audience is worthy of the singer's self-immolation and sacrifice. At other times the audience is passive, unappreciative, and unworthy: she talks scornfully of an acquaintance whose favorite part of the operas are the intervals; and we see her hold in contempt the stagehand in the recital hall, who neither knows nor cares about the art being created on the stage within earshot.

McNally best dramatizes the capacity of an audience to be moved by the artificially distilled expressive powers of the singer's voice and emotions channeled through the composer's music when Callas herself listens to Tony Candolino sing "Ricondita armonia." To the tenor's disappointment, after he has finished singing, she says only

"That was beautiful. I have nothing more to say. That was beautiful" (44). Being an audience member, being the recipient of the imagined emotions of Cavaradossi for Tosca as channeled through the voice and soul of the tenor as she never was when she played Tosca herself ("I was always backstage preparing for my entrance" [45]), Callas is, for one of the rare moments in the play, left speechless. And she stumbles awkwardly from that moment—a moment that demonstrates why, from an audience's point of view, the singer's art is worthwhile—to the unexpected admission that "It's a terrible career, actually. I don't know why I bothered" (45).

Through her pedagogical encounters with Sophie and Tony, Callas teaches both the students and the audience what it takes to become an effective singing actor. One must have suffered sufficiently to provide the emotional raw material for embodying the character's emotion. One must be willing to re-experience the most difficult times of one's life over and over again, with all of the focused and distilled intensity of the first experience. One must be willing to display one's most private feelings and experiences in public, both to an uncaring and ungrateful audience (personified, in *Master Class*, by the stagehand) and to an attentive and appreciative public that demands that each performance be yet another self-consuming and self-consumed display of re-experienced emotional agonies. And, finally, becoming a singing actor requires the singer to turn him- or herself into an artificial being, in part because the medium of musical and theatrical expression is so highly conventionalized and artificial and in part because of the cutthroat world of the operatic profession. One must, in short, play the part of the diva to be a diva; one must become a monster of egotism, selfishness, competitiveness, and vindictiveness, capable of cutting a swathe for oneself in the world of managers, conductors, directors, claques, and other divas, in order to get the opportunity to practice one's art. And, by practicing one's art, by dredging up every life experience and emotion in the service of the drama, and the dramatic character, and the music, one self-destructs, consuming irreversibly the raw material of the art in the very act of making the art. Becoming the diva leaves little more than dry tinder; singing sets the tinder alight, burning with a brilliant flame before the audience, until all that is left are ashes, thorns, and nails.

And so we see Maria Callas through the play: a brilliant actress still, still wearing her all-too-public life's pain on her sleeve, still grabbing the spotlight, indulging her ego, destroying with a glance or a quip everyone around her. And when she finally sings, the stage directions record, "What comes out is a cracked and broken thing" (47).[3]

By the middle of the second act, after Callas has coached two singers and driven a third from the stage, we have learned about the paradoxes of acting contained within the diva's craft, and we have come to some understanding of how this craft calls upon the singer to create a particular performative persona and to put that persona to the service of the self-consuming art of singing. Callas, in her roundabout and often contradictory way, explains these principles to us as she coaches Sophie and Tony, and she demonstrates, in her abominably egotistical behavior, what she has become in service of this art. But it not until the final third of the play, when she coaches Sharon Graham, that we see the means by which a younger singer can put these principles into practice, that we see a singer who can become, potentially at least, another Callas and, in this instance, chooses not to.

Sharon has returned to the recital stage after vomiting in fear and humiliation, determined now to prove herself. Callas humiliates her and browbeats her into acting and not just singing the aria, as she did with Sophie and Tony. But here, as we watch, the Stanislavskian exercises and the Strasbergian emotional memory substitutions begin to work. Callas insists that everything be concrete, specific: the letter from Macbeth that Lady Macbeth reads, in unsung speech before the recitative, must be real, and not imagined ("I don't want pretending. You're not good enough. I want truth [46]); the news of Duncan's imminent arrival comes not from 'someone' but from 'a servant'" (51). When Sharon hesitates between the recitative and the aria, Callas, swept up in the flow of the drama and encouraging Sharon to be swept up too, insists "don't even think of stopping! You are Lady Macbeth!" (48). After the aria, with the news of Duncan's arrival, the emotional identification of Sharon with Lady Macbeth is, with Callas's coaching, nearly complete:

Maria: How does that make her feel?
Soprano: Happy?

Maria: Don't keep looking at me for answers, Sharon. Tell me, show me.
    Vite, vite!
Soprano: Really happy.
Maria: Love happy? Christmas morning happy?
Soprano: Murder happy!
Maria: Ah! And what is she going to do about it?
Soprano: She's going to sing a cabaletta!
Maria: She's going to kill the king! Do you know what that means?
Soprano: Yes, it's terrible.
Maria: Not to her! Do you believe women can have balls, Sharon?
Soprano: Some women. Yes, I do!
Maria: Verdi is daring you to show us yours, Sharon. Will you do it?
Soprano: Yes! (51–52).

The stakes of the scene, the stakes of the act of performing itself, have become, for Sharon, nearly like those for Callas. "This isn't just an opera. This is your life," Callas insists (50). "Is there anything you would kill for, Sharon," she asks her, suggesting "A man, a career?" (53). "You have to listen to something in yourself to sing this difficult music," she insists, suggesting that the characters she has sung, and the characters of the classical tragedies of her native Greece—Medea, Electra, Klytemnestra—were real people, to whom she has a real connection:

Maria: These people really existed. Medea, Lady Macbeth. Or don't you
    believe that? Eh? This is all make-believe to you?
Soprano: I've never really thought about it.
Maria: That's because you're young. You will. In time. Know how much
    suffering there can be in store for a woman (53).

As Sharon sings, she feels in her soul, her body, and her voice the connection that Callas insists is the true art of the diva. And she is told, and undoubtedly understands, the life, emotions, and experience to which the singing actor's art must be connected: one in which she is capable of feeling that she *could* kill for a man or a career, where in time she will know how much suffering is in store for her, where she can not only believe in Medea or Lady Macbeth but can feel so strong a kinship with them that she can *become* them, emotionally and viscerally. Sharon, unlike Sophie and Tony, is capable of learning the lessons that Callas has to teach.

After Sharon finishes singing the complete aria and cabaletta, Callas, coming out of her reverie/flashback sequence, dismisses Sharon's professional prospects, damning her with the faint praise:

I think you should work on something more appropriate for your limitations. Mimi or Micaela maybe. But Lady Macbeth, Norma, I don't think so. These roles require something else. Something. How shall I say this? Something special. Something that can't be taught or passed on or copied or even talked about. Genius. Inspiration. A gift of god. Some recompense for everything else (61).

Sharon, in tears, responds:

I wish I'd never done this. I don't like you. You can't sing anymore and you're envious of anyone younger who can. You just want us to sing like you, recklessly, and lose our voices in ten years like you did. Well, I won't do it. I don't want to. I don't want to sing like you. I hate people like you. You want to make the world dangerous for everyone just because it was for you (61).

Sharon clearly wants to get back at Callas for her condescension. But there is more to her response than this. Sharon sees in Callas's cruelty the more important truth of the diva's art: that this type of art exacts too high a price, that one would not wish upon oneself the experiences and suffering that could generate such art, and that creating art from such personal and emotional raw materials is self-consuming, and ultimately destroys the medium of the art—the singer's voice. Sharon leaves the stage; Callas brushes off the confrontation, withdraws into the shell of her professional persona, utters a few platitudes about art and, saying "well, that's that" (62), brings both the master class and *Master Class* to a close.

Throughout the play, McNally has been putting forth as his hypothesis the myth of Callas the diva: she so channels her own life and emotions into her singing and acting; she so fully becomes a conduit for her own sorrows and the object of projection for the fantasies and emotions of her audiences that she has ruined her voice and withered into a cruel and egotistical if magnificent monster, a *monstre sacre*. Sharon's defection at the end only confirms the hypothesis and elevates the diva to an even-greater level: a figure of sublime loneliness, shunned as a pariah, so monstrous that she can be watched in awe but is too horrifying to be emulated.

The dramaturgical mastery of *Master Class* lies in its twin strategies for representing Callas as a dramatic character. For, in watching her teach, we see the monster she has become; and in learning *what* she teaches—the practices of personal, emotional-based acting that she teaches unsuccessfully to Sophie and Tony and successfully if Pyrrhically to Sharon—we learn how she has become that person. We see less the genuine person and more the persona that Callas has created for herself and that has been created for her: the diva. From the moment that Callas singles out a member of the audience to demonstrate how "It's important to have a look" (3), we see the theatricality, the performativity of the diva's persona. "This isn't a freak show. I'm not a performing seal," she tells Sophie, explaining that her fabled fieriness is not a performance but an ingrained part of her identity: "My fire comes from here, Sophie. It's mine. It's not for sale. It's not for me to give away. Even if I could, I wouldn't. It's who I am. Find out who you are. That's what this is all about. Eh?" (8). And yet Callas *is* a freak, a performing seal.[4] Within Callas's talents as a self-creator, within the persona that she has forged from her status as diva ("Never miss an opportunity to theatricalize," she tells Sharon [35]), everything is a performance. Acting, even when acting means surrendering to a character and effectively becoming that character, never entails the loss of self; indeed, it is where the performative self is created and articulated. As the stage director Visconti tells her (in the first-act flashback sequence), "You are not a village girl. You are Maria Callas playing a village girl" (24). Callas's "performance" as teacher of a master class *is* Callas. The diva uses herself to perform; consequently she only *is* when she performs.

And so it is—or should be—with McNally's drama: We see what she has become and we learn the process by which she became this way. But this is, of course, not the entire play, nor is the master class, despite the play's title, the only narrative and dramaturgical means by which the playwright shows us Callas's character. McNally has demonstrated for us what she has become and taught us the process of acting that has made her this way—one that demands that she wear her emotions on her sleeve and transmit her own life and suffering into her performances through her body and voice on stage. What we do not know—and what opera queens cannot know about a diva, except through gossip columns and the fanciful projections of their own imaginations—is the life lived, the nature of the actual sufferings that the singer transmutes into her performances.

The genius of *Master Class* is that, once we have seen what Callas has become and learned how she used (and used up) her life to get this way, we don't actually *need* to know the life that she lived. But this is precisely what McNally gives us, in the most theatrically stunning sequences of the play: the flashback fantasy sequences, to the accompaniment of Callas's live recordings of the arias that the student singers are singing. These sequences—brilliant as they are in performance, affording an opportunity for the actor to jump back and forth between Callas's student years and her triumphant debuts and between her public and private lives—belong to two other genres of play entirely. One genre is the autobiographical one-hander (such as the Lillian Hellman vehicle that Zoe Caldwell played a few years before she created the role of Callas in *Master Class*), in which the historical figure, through some theatrical pretense (Emily Dickinson inviting us in as neighbors to share her recipes, Truman Capote speaking into a tape recorder for the benefit of a journalist) retells and relives formative events from his or her life.

The other genre to which the flashback sequences of *Master Class* belongs is, arguably, the largest segment of American twentieth-century dramatic writing, what might best be called the "psychotherapeutic whodunit." In such plays, a protagonist's tragic agony or a family's crippling dysfunction can be traced, as in the Freudian psychoanalytical model, to a single, traumatic event, real or imagined, that is concealed from several of the characters and the audience until late in the play: Biff sees Willy with a prostitute in a cheap hotel in Boston; Mary Tyrone regresses to a point in her life before she discovered her husband to be an alcoholic and, more significantly, before the infant Eugene died of the infection given to him by his older brother Jamie; George and Martha "kill off" the child which the audience and Nick discover to have been invented by them; Dodge and Bradley narrate the story of the child buried in the backyard.

The flashback sequences in *Master Class* satisfy the whodunit energies generated by the theories of acting taught and practiced by Callas in the real-time framework of the play. If Callas is indeed transforming her real-life suffering, to which she casually alludes repeatedly in her teaching, then the audience naturally desires to learn more about these traumatic experiences: Callas proving herself to her teacher, Callas's La Scala debut, her final performances at La Scala in defiance of the general manager who was firing her, the patronage of Battista Meneghini, and her abusive relationship with Onassis. Moreover, the flashback sequences confirm the ways that Callas's personal emotions—shame, desire, vindictiveness, revenge— are channeled into her singing. Just as Lady Macbeth invites the unholy spirit to enter her body, Callas invites the voices of her own life to enter her, through Verdi's "infernal music," to "Come, fill me with your malevolence" (55). As the house lights in La Scala come up as Callas finishes her *La Somnambula* aria on the stage of La Scala, she is able to reverse the audience's vampiric gaze, to see the eyes of the viewers devouring her performance, and can declare, "My revenge, my triumph are complete" (29).

The logic of the standard American dramaturgical master narrative demands that the audience know the biographical causes of characterological effects. For an audience, to understand the formative traumas is to know the character; for a character, to face the cause is to begin to heal; and, for character and audience alike, theatrically reliving these traumas is both a form of purgation and a fulfillment of the play's dramaturgical logic. In *Master Class*, the traumatic event to which the whodunit logic of the play points turns out to be a familiar one in American drama: Callas, having been told by Onassis that the greatest gift she can give him is a child, announces that she is pregnant and is now told by him that she must get rid of the child. As in *Long Day's Journey into Night, Desire Under the Elms, Who's Afraid of Virginia Woolf, The American Dream, Buried Child, Talley's Folly,* and countless lesser American plays, the central hidden trauma of the play turns out to be female fertility; the missing center of the play and its character turns out to be, as it is in so many plays, the missing, dead, murdered, unconceived, or aborted baby. Underneath a fascinating metatheatrical drama about art lies a far more conventional American "dead baby" drama. We discover that Callas, the object of the opera queen's emulation and envy, is herself consumed with envy; and the object of her envy is something common both to American drama and to the mythology of male homosexuality: the womb.

In exploring the phenomenon of the diva, the play's own logic asks us to resist such easy answers. Callas was willing to create art from the material of her life at great cost. We learn how she did so, and we see the cost. If *Master Class* is indeed about art and its making out of life, then, ironically, we need to see the life *only* through the art. But in the flashback sequences and in their reversion to the traditional dead-baby trope, the playwright gives us too much. The sequences are arguably more than just a violation of the playwright's own metatheatrical fiction and more than just a deviation from his chosen dramaturgical structure in favor of a return to the more traditional structural conventions of the psychotherapeutic whodunit: they are a violation of the theories of art explored in the play. The flashbacks effectively turn the playwright, and the audience, into opera queens: they not only allow us, like the opera queen, to imagine that the person's real pain can be heard in the diva's voice; they materially confirm that the pain and its origins is everything we imagine it to be. In narrating and reenacting her life to sounds of her own voice singing Adina or Lady Macbeth on a recording, Callas is effectively lip-synching her own life, just as Stephen lip-synchs to Callas's Violetta at the end of *The Lisbon Traviata*. Callas not only fulfills the opera queen's myth of the diva; in *Master Class* the queen of opera demonstrably becomes an opera queen herself.

Notes

1.   Virtually every conventional twentieth-century play asks an audience to efface its existence, to pretend that it is not in a theatre: to pretend that the stage is not a stage but is an estate in Russia, a tenement in Brooklyn, or an apartment in New Orleans; and to pretend that the audience itself is invisible and incorporeal, voyeurs to the fiction of a life unfolding on the stage. Even in Pirandello's *Six Characters in Search of an Author*, which dispenses with one layer of fiction (the stage represents a stage and the auditorium represents an auditorium), the audience present in that auditorium must pretend that they are not there, that the auditorium is empty, that the performance they are attending is actually a rehearsal before empty seats.

2.   The phenomenon of homosexual identification with the performer is dramatized in *The Kiss of the Spider Woman*, McNally's adaptation of Manuel Puig's novel for the musical stage. Molina, the homosexual pederast and movie buff, displaces his artistic expressiveness onto his fantasy film actress just as the opera

queen displaces his own emotional expressiveness into the throat of the diva. While Aurora performs her song-and-dance numbers (in Molina's fantasy projections) downstage, Molina, seated upstage in his jail cell, moves his lips and silently gestures, mirroring Aurora's words and gestures.

3. In this, McNally has cleverly found a way to compensate for the impossibility of casting an actress who can actually *sing* like Callas; the role was written for an actress—Zoe Caldwell—who is not a singer.

4. And she demonstrates repeatedly (and demonstrated only a few seconds before) that fieriness and temperamentality are character traits only insofar as they put into action, and that a diva can put them into action at will. Sophie has boasted that her own Greek and Italian heritage has given her a fiery temperament. Callas asks:

Maria: *Do something fiery.*
Soprano: *I can't. Not just like that. No one can.*
Maria: *WHERE IS MY FOOTSTOOL?*
Soprano: *Well, I guess some people can (8).*

5. It is not unusual for male playwrights, of whatever sexual orientation, to turn to issues of fertility when they invent formative traumas for their female characters. A key example is the South African playwright Athol Fugard: in *The Road to Mecca*, his first (and to date only) play with two principal female characters and only a subsidiary male role, he needed to invent a biographical source for Elsa's dramatic crisis (the other principal female character, Helen, was drawn from life), and chose to have her reveal to Helen, in the play's final moments, that she had just had an abortion.

Works Cited

Koestenbaum, Wayne. *The Queen's Throat: Opera, Homosexuality, and the Mystery of Desire*. New York: Poseidon Press, 1993.

McNally, Terrence. *Master Class*. New York: Penguin Books, 1995.

———. *Three Plays by Terrence McNally: The Lisbon Traviata, Frankie and Johnny in the Clair de Lune, It's Only a Play*. New York: Penguin Books, 1990.

Selected Bibliography

Primary Sources
Plays (Date of first professional production in parentheses)

The Roller Coaster. Columbia Review. Spring 1960: 42–60.

This Side of the Door, 1962.

The Lady of the Camellias (1963): adaptation by Giles Cooper based on the play by Dumas fils.

And Things That Go Bump in the Night (1964) [previously There Is Something Out There (1962)]. New York: Dramatists Play Service, 1966.

Tour (1967) in Apple Pie: Three One Act Plays. New York: Dramatists Play Service.

*Next (1967), revised version (1968, 1969) in Apple Pie: Three One Act Plays. New York: Dramatists Play Service, 1969.

*Noon (1968)

*Botticelli (televised 1968)

*¡Cuba Si! (1968)

*Sweet Eros (1968)

*Witness (1968)

*Bringing It All Back Home (1969, New Haven; 1972, New York)

Last Gasps (televised 1969) in ¡Cuba Si!, Bringing It All Back Home, Last Gasps. New York: Dramatists Play Service, 1970.

Where Has Tommy Flowers Gone? (1971) New York: Dramatists Play Service, 1972.

Let It Bleed (in City Stops, Bronx Community College, 1972)

*Whiskey (1973)

* Bad Habits (1974)

*The Ritz [originally The Tubs (Yale, 1974)], (1975)

It's Only a Play (1985) [originally titled, Broadway, Broadway (1978)], in Three Plays by Terrence McNally: The Lisbon Traviata, Frankie and Johnny in the Clair de Lune, It's Only a Play. New York: Plume, 1990.

Frankie and Johnny in the Clair de Lune (1987), in Three Plays by Terrence McNally: The Lisbon Traviata, Frankie and Johnny in the Clair de Lune, It's Only a Play. New York: Plume, 1990.

*Andre's Mother (1988)

*Street Talk (1988)

The Lisbon Traviata (1985, revised1989) in Three Plays by Terrence McNally: The Lisbon Traviata, Frankie and Johnny in the Clair de Lune , It's Only a Play, New York: Plume, 1990.

*Prelude & Liebestod (1989)

Lips Together, Teeth Apart (1991), New York: Plume, 1992.

---

*in Terrence McNally: 15 Short Plays . Lyme, NH: Smith and Kraus, 1994.

*The Wibbly, Wobbly, Wiggly Dance That Cleopatterer Did (1993)
*Hidden Agendas
A Perfect Ganesh (1993) in Love! Valour! Compassion! and A Perfect Ganesh, New
    York: Plume, 1995.
Love! Valour! Compassion! (1994) in Love!Valour!Compassion! and A Perfect Ganesh,
    New York: Plume, 1995.
Master Class (1995). New York: Plume, 1995.
Dusk (1996) in By the Sea, By the Sea, By the Beautiful Sea.

Books for musicals

Here's Where I Belong (1968). Music by Robert Waldman. Based on John Steinbeck's
    East of Eden.
The Rink (1984). Music by John Kander; lyrics by Fred Ebb. New York: French's Musi-
    cal Library, 1985.
Kiss of the Spider Woman (1993). Adaptation of the novel by Manuel Puig, with music
    by John Kander, lyrics by Fred Ebb.
Ragtime (1996). Adaptation of the novel by E.L. Doctorow, with music by Stephen
    Flaherty and lyrics by Lynne Ahrens.

Screenplays

The Ritz, 1976.
Frankie and Johnny, 1991
Love! Valour! Compassion!, 1996
A Perfect Ganesh, forthcoming.

Teleplays

Botticelli, 1968
Last Gasps, 1969.
The Five Forty-Eight, from the story by John Cheever, 1979.
Mama Malone series, 1983.
Andre's Mother, 1990.

Prose (Selected)

"Theatre Isn't All on Broadway." New York Times, 28 April 1974: 2:1.
"The Ritz on Stage and Screen." Dramatists Guild Quarterly 14 (Spring 1977), 26:32–36.
Introduction to The Callas Legacy by John Ardoin. NY: Charles Scribners, 1991, pp.xi–xiv.
Preface to Terrence McNally:15 Short Plays Lyme, NH: Smith and Kraus, 1994.
"A Few Words of Introduction" in Three Plays by Terrence McNally: The Lisbon
    Traviata, Frankie and Johnny in the Clair de Lune, It's Only a Play. New York:
    Plume, 1990.

Interviews/Profiles

Bryer, Jackson R., ed. The Playwright's Art: Conversations with Contemporary Ameri-
    can Playwrights. New Brunswick, NJ: Rutgers University Press, 1995.
DiGaetani, John L. "Terrence McNally." A Search for a Postmodern Theater: Inter-
    views with Contemporary Playwrights. Westport, CT: Greenwood Press, 1991.
Drukman, Steven. "Terrence McNally." Speaking on Stage: Interviews with Contempo-
    rary American Playwrights. Eds. Philip Kolin and Colby Kullman. University of
    Alabama Press, 1996.
"Edward Albee in Conversation with Terrence McNally." Dramatists Guild Quarterly 22
    (Summer 1985): 12–23.

"Frank Rich in Conversation with Terrence McNally." *Dramatists Guild Quarterly* 24
    (Autumn 1987): 11–29.
"Humor: A Cool Discussion." *Dramatists Guild Quarterly* 14 (Winter 1978): 8–25. [with
    Russell Baker, Jules Feiffer, Bruce Jay Friedman]
"Landmark Symposium: *Tea and Sympathy*." *Dramatists Guild Quarterly* 19 (1983) 11–
    27. [discussion with Elia Kazan]
Rosen, Carol. "Terrence McNally." *TheaterWeek*, 27 February 1995, 12–24.
"Sex and the Theatre: Doing What Comes Naturally." *Dramatists Guild Quarterly* 17
    (1980): 22–33. [symposium with Robert Anderson]
Zinman, Toby Silverman. "The Muses of Terrence McNally." *American Theatre.* March
    1995: 12–17.

Selected Secondary Sources

Abel, Sam. "The Death of Queens: *The Lisbon Traviata* Controversy and Gay Male
    Representation in the Mainstream Theatre." *Theatre History Studies* 16 (1996).
Barnes, Clive. "Making the Most of the Ritz Steam Bath." *New York Times*, 21 Janu-
    ary 1975, as reprinted in *New York Theater Critics Reviews*, vol. 36 (1975): 377.
Bersani, Leo. *Homos.* Cambridge, Mass.: Harvard UP, 1995.
Brustein, Robert. "Aspects of Love and Compassion." *The New Republic*, 3 April
    1995: 30–31.
———. "Yuppie Realism, Continued." *The New Republic*, 21 October 1991: 28–29.
Canby, Vincent. "McNally, True, but Vaguely Neo-Chekhovian" *The New York Times*, 6
    November 1994: 5, 32.
Clum, John M. *Acting Gay: Male Homosexuality in Modern Drama*, rev. ed. New York:
    Columbia UP, 1994.
Collins, Glenn. "A Comic Triumph as a Tragic Callas Worshipper." *New York Times*, 14
    June 1989: C19.
Crutchfield, Will. "Dishing About Divas and Other Opera Chat." *New York Times*, 4
    June 1989: II, 5+.
Disch, Thomas M. "The Lisbon Traviata." *The Nation*, 18 December 1989: 766–7.
Doty, Alexander. *Making Things Perfectly Queer: Interpreting Mass Culture.* Minneapo-
    lis: U of Minnesota Press, 1993.
Drukman, Steven. "Gay-Gazing at *The Lisbon Traviata*, or: How Are Things in *Tosca*,
    Norma?" *Theatre Topics* 5.1 (1995): 23–34.
Feingold, Michael. "Camp Followers." *Village Voice*, 13 June 1989: 97.
Franklin, Nancy. "McNally Men, Wasserstein Women." *The New Yorker*, 14 November
    1994.
Gerard, Jeremy. "Sex! Velour! Compulsion!" *Variety*, 21 November 1994: 40.
———. "Master Class." *Variety*, 6 November 1996: 78.
Gilbert, Reed. "That's Why I Go to the Gym: Sexual Identity and the Body of the Male
    Performer." *Theatre Journal* 4 (1994): 477–88.
Gottfried, Martin. "Throwing in the Towel." *New York Post*, 21 January 1975, as re-
    printed in *New York Theater Critics Reviews*, vol. 36 (1975): 376.
Gussow, Mel. "Agony and Ecstasy of an Opera Addiction." *New York Times*, 7 June
    1989: 21.
———. "A New, Non-Violent Ending for 'Lisbon Traviata'." *New York Times*, 1 Novem-
    ber 1989: 22.
———. "Stage: 'Lisbon Traviata,' Tale of Two Opera Fans." *New York Times*, 19 June
    1985: III, 14.
Humm. "Frankie and Johnny in the Clair de Lune." *Variety*, 11 November 1987: 90.
Kaufman, David. "Frankie and Johnny Are Modern Lovers." *New York Times*, 11 Octo-
    ber 1987: sec. 2, 3 &14.
Klein, Alvin. "McNally's Plays Take Diverse Paths." *New York Times* 19 November
    1989: 21, 25.

Koestenbaum, Wayne. *The Queen's Throat: Opera, Homosexuality, and the Mystery of Desire*. New York: Poseidon Press, 1993.

Kramer, Mimi. "The Manhattan Traviata." *The New Yorker,* 19 June 1989: 74–6.

Lehman, Peter. *Running Scared: Masculinity and the Representation of the Male Body*. Philadelphia: Temple UP, 1993.

Marowitz, Charles. "Los Angeles in Review: *The Lisbon Traviata.*" *Theatre Week,* 31 December 1990: 38–39.

Montgomery, Benilde. "*Lips Together, Teeth Apart:* Another Version of Pastoral." *Modern Drama* 36 (1993): 547–55.

"Naked Truths." *The New Yorker,* 13 February 1995, 32–33.

Novick, Julius. "Ave Maria." *Village Voice,* 2 July 1985: 95–6.

Rich, Frank. "After Sex, What?" *New York Times,* 25 October 1987: C23.

———. "Struggling to Love, but Aware of the Odds." *New York Times,* 26 June 1991, as reprinted in *New York Theater Critics Reviews,* vol. 52 (1991): 183.

Richards, David. "Two Shapes of Comedy—Tragic and Spoof." *New York Times,* 13 July 1991: 145–47.

———. "In the Hearts and Minds of Men Who Love Men" in *The New York Times,* 2 November 1994: C13–C15.

Roman, David, "'It's My Party and I'll Die if I Want To!': Gay Men, AIDS, and the Circulation of Camp in U.S. Theatre." *Theatre Journal* 44 (October 1992):305– 328.

Rosenberg, Scott. "Playwright Dreams of the Road." *San Francisco Examiner,* 21 October 1990: E-1.

Sarris, Andrew. "Putting on The Ritz." *Village Voice,* 23 August 1976: 117.

Sedgwick, Eve Kosofsky. *Tendencies*. Durham, N.C.: Duke UP, 1993.

Shewey, Don. *Out Front*. New York: Grove Press, 1988.

Simon, John. "All Wet." *New York Magazine,* 15 July 1985: 67–9.

———. "Anti-Romances." *New York Magazine,* 19 June 1989: 71–3.

———. "Bath House Bathos." *New York Magazine,* 3 February 1975: 65.

———. "The Plot Thins." *New York Magazine* 20 January 1986: 56–57.

———. "Saucy! Schmaltzy! Slow Moving!" in *New York Magazine,* 14 November 1994: 79–80.

———. "Something Borrowed, Something Blah." *New York Magazine,* 13 November 1989: 130–1.

Straub, Deborah. "McNally, Terrence." *Contemporary Authors*. New Revision Series, vol. 2. Detroit, Michigan: Gale Research Co., 1962–81: 457–58.

Torrens, James S. "A Perfect Ganesh," *America,* 14 August 1993: 22.

Weston, Kath. *Families We Choose: Lesbians, Gays, Kinship*. New York: Columbia UP, 1991.

Winer, Laurie. "In the End, 'Love!' Prayers Are Answered" in *The Los Angeles Times,* 15 November 1994: 23.

Zinman, Toby. "Master Class." *Variety,* 6 March 1995: 72.

Contributors

Sam Abel teaches in the Department of Drama at Dartmouth College. He is the author of *Opera in the Flesh: Sexuality in Operatic Performance* (Westview Press) and has published articles in *Theatre History Studies, Theatre Annual, Theatre Topics, Opera News, Western European Stages, The Journal of Popular Culture,* and several anthologies.

John Ardoin is music critic of *The Dallas Morning News* and author of *The Callas Legacy, Callas at Juilliard,* and *The Furtwangler Record.* He is currently in Russia at work on a book about the Bolshoi Ballet.

Helen T. Buttel, Professor Emeritus, taught drama and film at Beaver College and continues to teach film in their Community Scholars Program. She has published most recently in *Film Quarterly* and *Journal of Modern Literature.*

John M. Clum is Professor of English and Professor of the Practice of Theater at Duke University. He is the author of a number of books and essays on twentieth-century American and British drama and gay studies. His most recent book is *Acting Gay: Male Homosexuality in Modern Drama* (Columbia, 1992; rev.ed.1994). He is also a playwright whose work has been performed recently in Washington, Baltimore, his native Durham, N.C., and London.

Steven Drukman has written about the theatre for *The Village Voice, Theatre Journal, TDR, Theatre Topics* and many other journals and publications. He is the Contributing Editor of *American Theatre* magazine and the theatre critic for *Artforum.* He teaches in the undergraduate Department of Drama at New York University. His interview with Terrence McNally can be found in *Speaking on Stage* (University of Alabama Press).

Cary M. Mazer is Associate Professor of English and Chair of the Theatre Arts Program at the University of Pennsylvania. He is author of *Shakespeare Refashioned: Elizabethan Plays on Edwardian Stages*, and articles on Victorian and Edwardian theatre, Shakespeare in performance, and nineteenth and twentieth-century drama and theatre. He directs plays at Penn, has served as a dramaturg at People's Light & Theatre Company in Malvern, PA, and is theatre critic for *City Paper*.

Benilde Montgomery is Assistant Professor of Drama and Coordinator of Drama and Dance at Dowling College, Oakdale, New York. His work has appeared in *Irish Renaissance Annual, Journal of American Academy of Religions, Eighteenth Century Studies*, and, most recently, *Modern Drama*.

Howard Stein, retired chair of the Oscar Hammerstein Center at Columbia University, continues to co-edit the annual *Best Short American Plays*. Most recently he has written on James Barrie for Scribner's *British Writers, Supplement III* and an essay on John Guare for another volume in this Garland series. Retired and enjoying it, he continues to work on his lifetime project, "Why Don't They Write Plays Like They Used To?"

Stephen Watt is Associate Professor of English at Indiana University in Bloomington. His books include, *Joyce, O'Casey, and the Irish Popular Theater* (1991) and, with Gary A. Richardson, *American Drama: Colonial to Contemporary* (Harcourt, 1995), and an anthology, *Marketing Modernisms*, ed. with Kevin J.H. Dettmar (University of Michigan, 1996).

Toby Silverman Zinman is Professor of English in the Humanities Division and Literary Manager of the Theatre Department at the University of the Arts in Philadelphia. She is also theatre critic for *Variety* and for Philadelphia's *City Paper*, and is a feature writer for

American Theatre. She is editor of *David Rabe: A Casebook* (Garland) and publishes and lectures internationally on contemporary drama.

Index

Schmitt